# RELIGION
# AND DOUBT:
## Toward a Faith of Your Own

Richard E. Creel

*Ithaca College*

PRENTICE-HALL, INC., Englewood Cliffs, New Jersey

*Library of Congress Cataloging in Publication Data*

Creel, Richard E., (date).
   Religion and doubt.

   Bibliography: p.
   1. Religion. I. Title.
BL48.C725    200'.1'9      76-23102
ISBN 0-13-771949-3
ISBN 0-13-771931-0 pbk.

10  9  8  7  6  5  4  3  2  1

PRENTICE-HALL INTERNATIONAL, INC., *London*
PRENTICE-HALL OF AUSTRALIA, PTY., LIMITED, *Sydney*
PRENTICE-HALL OF CANADA, LTD., *Toronto*
PRENTICE-HALL OF INDIA PRIVATE LIMITED, *New Delhi*
PRENTICE-HALL OF JAPAN, INC., *Tokyo*
PRENTICE-HALL OF SOUTHEAST ASIA PTE. LTD., *Singapore*
WHITEHALL BOOKS LIMITED, *Wellington, New Zealand*

*To Diane—truly my other half*

*To my parents, Richard and Grace—for a lifetime*
*of love and encouragement*

*and*

*To my brother, Dan—a fellow seeker and finder*

# Contents

v

# Foreword

When I was asked if I would prepare a foreword for Richard Creel's book, my reaction was one of surprise, delight, and hard-nosed realism: what an unknown author does not need is another unknown author to introduce his book.

But then, quite by accident, I discovered that what I had thought was spelled "forward" is spelled "foreword"! This put the matter in an entirely different light; in effect, I was being given the opportunity of getting in the *first word*. This is a point of chivalry, an advantage seldom granted by philosopher or theologian to a layperson. So, on behalf of my fellow readers, I make the following comments.

*The First Word*—is a complaint, not about Richard Creel, but about philosophers and theologians in general. They dig and dabble in the ultimate truths and in the precious mysteries of life; indeed, they discover and package these truths in such precise, concrete structures of logic and language that they become almost forever sealed from the throngs of would-be seekers. Hence, what philosophers and theologians need is a translator. That is the complaint.

Suddenly along comes Richard Creel, loping over the hills by Lake Cayuga's waters. He actually sits down with his readers and chats! Without fuss or pretense, he tackles topics that ordinarily leave us tongue-tied. He slips us questions and some of the answers, till, presently, lo; we discover we are acquiring for ourselves some of the tools of philosophical and theological thought. Indeed, we find that to grow in personal faith is something more than to study religion.

*The Second Word*—is that I had a better title for this book! It should have been called *Dandelions of Faith.*

"But," says the author, who is trying to think like his publisher (very important!), "no one will understand from *that* title what my book is about. People do not naturally equate dandelions with religion, let alone doubt."

"A pity."

"Explain the metaphor."

"Dandelions . . . You mean dandelions??? Well, it's like this. There is a thing about dandelions. We uproot them, we poison them, we try to get them out of our manicured lawns . . . but they persist, are absolutely indestructible, will appear even in the cracks of a concrete superhighway. And that is the way also with this thing called faith, this thing called religion, and this thing called doubt. Dandelions are simply descriptive of our human and religious predicament."

"Predicament??!"

"Ah, *hah* . . . don't you see?

1. No matter how hard institutional religions attempt to codify and structure our faith, we persist in heretical intuitions and doubts, and

2. no matter how hard secular society would infest us with doubt and relativity, there is something deep within us which hungers for truths and patterns, for forms of eternal meaning."

"And so . . .?"

"And so what seems inevitable is that our faith, our doubts, and, to a certain extent, our religions are like the dandelions, which refuse to be exterminated, and which have a beauty and a freedom all their own.

"Moreover, our personal faith and our understanding of religious phenomena is usually a hodge-podge of experience and perception; it is not a well-groomed, manicured lawn. I suppose, systematically and theologically speaking, we are a Lovable Mess.

"Hence, I propose that, if our very own personal faith is alive and kicking, we are not like a lawn but a meadow, albeit possibly or properly fenced with tradition, logic, or dogma. And within this meadow there is a constant flowering of new thoughts and intuitions which give color and pattern. And after the blossom, the seed which floats on tails of fluff from one meadow to the next—crazy, unsystematic . . . quite defying

> the logic and training and
> instincts of a theologian
> or a Vatican Council.''

"I think I'm getting lost in your meadow-phor!"

"Lost?? You can't be. You are the one who has gathered the dandelions. You have lined up the meadows of mind and spirit, and, theologically speaking, helped us to fence them in.

"What is more, Professor Creel—all metaphors aside—you have done it rather well . . . and we
Thank You.''

HARRIET CRAMTON
*Ithaca, New York*
1975

# Preface

There have been eras when it was easy to believe wholeheartedly in a particular world view. Medieval Europeans were largely persuaded by the Christian world view. Many middle twentieth-century Americans believe in a scientific-materialistic world view. Distinctive of such eras is the feeling of obviousness which attaches to the belief in question. As many medieval Europeans believed that the Christian view of the world was obviously true, many contemporary Americans believe that the truth of "the scientific world view" is obvious. Yet even in an era of faith there are doubters—not malicious or cynical people, but people who, for whatever reasons, are not easily convinced by the prevailing world view, or by the world view within which they have been reared. Perhaps you are such a person. Indeed, chances are that you are, for our own era of belief seems to be crumbling. On the one hand, science hasn't given us what we expected of it (indeed, some now perceive it as a Frankenstein monster). On the other hand, owing to communication and travel, we can hardly fail to be challenged by the discovery that there are numerous ways of looking at the world—ways among which we must choose because they conflict with, and even attack, one another. A natural response to this challenge is to attempt to study *all*

the alternatives in order to choose the true one and reject the false conten-
ders. Such an endeavor quickly becomes so perplexing and exhausting that
one is tempted to drop the whole enterprise as hopeless. Yet we cannot
escape from the nagging desire to have some sense of who we are, where
we have come from, and where we are going. Hence, a desperate decision to
become agnostic, to say, "I don't know and there is no way to find out, so
I'm going to quit trying!" is one of those resolves we rarely keep. Without
even realizing what is happening, we become involved in a debate or a book
or a thought that leads us right back to those central questions of religion:
Who am I? What is the nature of the reality within which I live and move
and have my being? How ought I to live my life? What is the meaning of my
death? These are the kinds of concerns which this book is about. My primary
concern, though, is not to *tell* you what others have said about these things,
but to involve you in the process of making up your own mind about them.
To be sure, I will expose you to the views of many writers in philosophy,
religion, and psychology, but my intention is not to teach you what they
say. Rather, it is to provoke you into reflection by means of what they say.
My sincerest wish is that you will quickly find yourself caught in the flow of
what is being said and pulled along by your own deep interest until you have
reached the end—an end that will prove to be a launching rather than a
stopping! In the process I hope you will have acquired a more profound
understanding of the nature of religion and some assistance in understanding
and furthering your own religious growth.

Speaking of which, I would like to mention some of the people who
have contributed to my religious growth by reading this volume and making
invaluable comments. Special thanks go to my wife, Diane, who found and
sanded many a rough spot, to Professor Julian Davies, O.F.M., whose
sensitivity and patience have helped me see clearly what before was only
a blur, and to Harriet Cramton, whose facility for linguistic playfulness has
saved me time and again from writing solemnly when I needn't. I am
indebted also to Professor Ming Chiu, Rev. Herman Eckelmann, Rev.
Robert J. Kaiser, Professor Michael Meilach, O.F.M., Professor James
Muyskens, Professor Robert Newman, Rev. Jack Taylor, Rev. Dale Winter,
and numerous others, especially students, who have discussed these issues
with me. Finally, how could I forget those wonderful people with the magic
fingers and the infinite patience—my secretaries and typists: Dottie Owens,
Ellen Lauricella, Margaret Treacy, and Linda Frank. Having long been
impressed by second editions, I hope that this volume will have a chance to
be rewritten in a few years and that *you* will have given me the benefit of
your own reactions to what I have to say. So let's get on with it!

RICHARD CREEL

# Why Study Religion?

## THREE IMPORTANT REASONS

There are many important reasons for studying religion, but three seem especially important. First, if to be well-educated means to be well-acquainted with the fundamental aspects of human existence, then it is simply impossible to be well-educated without acquiring a mature understanding of religion. Why? Because religion is one of the most *ancient, universal,* and *enduring* components of human existence.

Regarding its antiquity, as far back as we can trace human culture, we find evidences of religious beliefs and practices. The evidence, such as modes of burial and paintings on cave walls, is clear with regard to Cro-Magnon and Neanderthal humans, and is present possibly even earlier.[1] Though such evidence is subject to a wide range of interpretations, it does seem to indicate clearly that humans as much as 100,000 years ago were seeking more than survival and comfort and were sensitive to more than the pragmatic aspects of their experience. There seems to have been a mystic sense of kinship with nature and animals. There seem to have been rituals whereby values were preserved and the community related to a larger reality. There were paintings and statues rich in symbolic significance. There was belief in spirit powers and quite likely in survival of the dead. There appear to have been sacramental acts (perhaps involving the consumption of human brains and the special arrangement of human skulls!) by means of which an exalted sense of self was sought. Hence, ambiguous as the evidence may be, it does seem clear that quite early humans were not merely living in the world but were interpreting it, forging an understanding of it and in turn being forged by that understanding as it found its expression in rituals, dances, sacraments, art work, songs, and eventually creeds and codes.[2]

Religion is not, however, an ancient but isolated phenomenon. Today, as yesterday, no matter where we look on the face of the earth, we find that the people there have a religion—not always in a biblical sense, to be sure, but always in some sense. In Africa there is Islam; in Europe, Australia, and the Americas, there are Judaism and Christianity; in Asia and Japan there are Hinduism and Buddhism; and on each of these continents there are members of each of the other faiths named, plus devotees of additional faiths which are smaller in number, but often powerful in influence: for example, Sikhism, Shinto, Taoism, Confucianism, Unitarian-Universalism, and Baha'i.

Further, in spite of predictions that religion would be "outgrown" in this century—some have said that God died in the nineteenth century and religion was scheduled to die in the twentieth!—it is as vigorous as ever, almost like the mythical many-headed Hydra which sprouted two heads for each one cut off! Thus, there is no empirical reason to think that religion is on its way out of the human scene. Indeed, one of the things which seems to annoy the Russian Communists from time to time is the fact that religion in the Soviet Union has not disappeared on schedule. (Karl Marx, the founder of modern communism, predicted that once capitalism was replaced by socialism, religion would wither like a plant plucked from its native soil.) So, we read in the newspapers from time to time about renewed efforts by the Russian Communist party to discourage and root out religion. It will never succeed, of course, for even if it rids its nation of all Jews and Christians, there will still be at least one religion left. Which one? Communism itself! It may puzzle, even bother you that I call communism a religion, but as we shall see, after we have constructed a functional understanding of religion, something can be a religion without being based on the concept of a personal God. But more of that later. The main point now is that religion is as irrepressible, as natural to human existence, as are philosophy and art. Particular religions may come and go, even as particular styles of art and schools of philosophy do, but—as I shall argue in Chapters 3 and 4—religion itself will endure and thrive as long as people are human.

A second important reason for studying religion is to better understand and communicate with our contemporaries. The world is increasingly crowded because of population growth, and the population is increasingly mixed together by ease of travel and mass communication. Hence, the need to communicate in nonoffensive ways with people of persuasions other than our own is increasingly urgent. Among the most important things to know about a people in order to communicate effectively with them and to develop relations of mutual respect and appreciation are certainly their religious beliefs and practices. Why? First, because the religion of a people embodies and celebrates precisely those things that are most precious to them. Second, the religious beliefs and values of a people condition the very way they see the world and respond to it. These beliefs and values, writes W. C. Smith,

> matter not only in the sense that their adherent cherishes them, regarding them as supremely precious. More subtly and elementally, he thinks by means of them, feels in terms of them, and acts by them, and for them, and through them—even when he is thinking, feeling, and acting in the matters that we regard as political and economic.[3]

Later Smith adds that unless people "can learn to understand and to be loyal to each other across religious frontiers, unless we can build a world in which people profoundly of different faiths can live together and work together, then the prospects for our planet's future are not bright."[4] In order to understand another person, then, it is valuable, perhaps imperative, to understand his religion. Prudence requires it, and so does human solidarity.

The third reason for studying religion is the personal reason. Religion is directly and intensely concerned with issues that haunt all of us: meaning and meaninglessness, right and wrong, love and hate, community and loneliness, war and peace, life and death, illusion and reality. Hence, it is only natural that we should study religion not only out of intellectual curiosity and social responsibility but also out of personal passion; not only as an interesting diversion and an act of social prudence but also as an attempt to find or forge a viable understanding of ourselves and the reality of which we are a part. It is understandable, then, in the words of Huston Smith, that a living religion is not a "dull habit" but "an acute fever." "And whenever religion comes to life," he adds, "it displays a startling quality; it takes over. All else, while not silenced, becomes subdued and thrown without contest into a supporting role."[5]

## FAITH AS A SEED WITHIN

To be sure, not everyone is obsessed by religion. Some are hostile to it, some are indifferent, some are simply curious. Still, I believe, religious concerns are like seeds that lie dormant in all of us. In some of us they germinate earlier and in some of us later. (And in some, perhaps, not at all?) Where *you* are right now in your religious growth I do not know—you may

© 1960 United Feature Syndicate, Inc.

not be sure yourself. Is your primary attitude toward religion one of curiosity as to how people can get so excited about it? Or perhaps religion has developed into a curse and a plague, afflicting you with unanswered questions and unsatisfied yearnings? Or perhaps it is the greatest source of strength and happiness in your life? Wherever you are, it does seem true that much as we awaken socially and sexually, we also awaken religiously. And when we do, our religious concern "takes over." It becomes our ultimate concern because it is our concern about what is ultimate.

Why study religion, then? In order (1) to broaden and deepen our understanding of a fundamental aspect of human existence; (2) to better understand and communicate with our contemporaries; and (3) to respond personally to the ultimate issues that confront us each and all.

**Footnotes**

1. For an introduction to this fascinating aspect of human history, see the opening chapter, John B. Noss, "Religion in Prehistoric and Primitive Cultures," *Man's Religions,* 5th ed. (New York: Macmillan Publishing Co., Inc., 1974).

2. I say "eventually" creeds and codes because I suspect that a statement attributed to Arthur Darby Nock is more right than wrong: "Primitive religion is not believed. It is danced." Songs, dances, and rituals almost certainly preceded articulated creeds of belief and codes of behavior.

3. Wilfred Cantwell Smith, *The Faith of Other Men* (New York: Mentor Books, 1965), p. 96.

4. Ibid., p. 116.

5. Huston Smith, *The Religions of Man* (New York: Mentor Books, 1960), p. 10.

CHAPTER 2

# Approaches to Religion

QUESTIONS TO THINK ABOUT

- How does phenomenology of religion differ from comparative religion?
- How does "history of religions" in the broader, more recent sense differ from "history of religions" in the narrower, more familiar sense?
- What kinds of things do social scientists, such as the sociologist, the anthropologist, and the psychologist, try to discover about religions?
- What kinds of questions about religion fall outside the realm of the social sciences?
- How does philosophy of religion differ from theology?
- What are some characteristics of the existentialist approach to religion?
- If a person is personally committed to and involved in a particular religion, can he evaluate that religion fairly and adequately?
- If a person is *not* personally committed to and involved in a particular religion, can he evaluate that religion fairly and adequately?

Once you've decided that it is important to study religion, you might think, "Well, okay; I'll dive right in!" But it's not that simple. Where do you dive in? What is it you are going to dive into? And what kind of a dive are you going to take? That metaphor's beginning to crack, so let's drop it, but I'm sure you'll agree that in a book of this length not everything interesting and important about religion can be said. Hence, in order to get our bearings on this mammoth field of study, let's take a look at nine different ways of approaching it. Such an overview of contemporary approaches to religion will enable me to make more clear what we will and will not be doing in the remainder of this book, and it will make you knowledgeable as to where to turn regarding those aspects of religion I do not treat.

I hope my descriptions will give you a working sense of the richness and diversity of the approaches that can be taken to religion, but please keep in mind at all times that I am painting with a very broad brush, and am therefore leaving out a great deal of detail and nuance. Each of these approaches can be firmly distinguished from the others in broad terms, but among some of the approaches there is considerable overlap, and some of the differences are subtle. An examination of these subtle differences and areas of overlap belongs to a more technical book than this, so we shall not pursue these issues. All of these approaches can be connected in theory, however, and many of them are intimately related in practice. Indeed, each of these approaches, in my own opinion, makes a distinct and valuable contribution to the division of labor that is necessary for a comprehensive understanding of religion. Further, each approach provides a distinct and fascinating point of view from which to look at religion. If you do not get a sense of the excitement, value, and mystique of each approach, the fault is mine, and I urge you to turn to some of the books listed in the bibliography. Finally, you should be aware that some knowledgeable persons will find my descriptions controversial. That's okay with me as long as my descriptions enable *you* to enter the controversy! Now let's begin our overview.

## PHENOMENOLOGY OF RELIGION

*Phenomonology of religion* is above all a method for coping with a problem which besets us all. When dealing with familiar things and persons, we often discover in retrospect that we have attributed to them meanings that were not there. How many times a defensive reaction to what a friend or mate has said has proved unwarranted! How many times we have misjudged peoples' character on the basis of their appearance! If such things can happen so frequently with familiar objects and persons, how much more likely they are to happen when we are dealing with a foreign culture! You might be thinking, "Actually, we'd do better with a foreign culture because we would be more careful, realizing the difficulty of understanding its people and their culture correctly." There is something to that response, I agree, but it misses the more fundamental point that our most serious misinterpretations are not the result of not being careful; they happen because we fail to realize that we are systematically distorting what we are looking at by interpreting it automatically in terms of deeply ingrained preconceptions—preconceptions that are as spontaneously a part of us as our posture, gait, and style of speech.

Phenomenology, founded by Edmund Husserl, a nineteenth-century German philosopher, is a rigorous method designed to help us escape from our preconceptions in order that we might get to "the things themselves," without distortion, or at least with a minimum of distortion from our habitual ways of understanding the world. By "bracketing out" our preconceptions—something one doesn't learn to do overnight—we allow things to present themselves to us *as they really are.* By applying this method of study to a religion, we come to understand that particular religion as it is *in its actuality for its adherents,* and not merely as it appears to an outsider. We come to see and feel the world of nature through the "eyes" of those people, and we come to appreciate the religious significance of the objects and actions that make up their social world. Surely it is this kind of knowledge that we want of a religion, and not, as W. C. Smith puts it, the kind of knowledge a fly must have of goldfish in a bowl. To be sure, our anthropomorphic fly might learn a good deal about goldfish by wandering around the outside of the bowl and staring in. But that is not enough. Our goal, as Smith puts it, is "not only to ascertain the institutions, beliefs, and practices of a tradition but to ascertain also, if one can, what these things mean to those who participate in them."[1]

In addition to the hermeneutical task (that is, the task of interpreting accurately and fully what religious phenomena—divine beings, scriptures, rituals, sacraments, etc.—mean to their devotees), phenomenologists also endeavor by means of their method to "lay bare" or "disclose" the structures and essences of the specific religions they study, and ultimately, the general essence of religion itself. Because these structures and essences manifest themselves in and through the externals of a religion, they can be apprehended accurately and deeply only by a properly unbiased and sensitive approach—and that is what phenomenology is about. Understandably, then, the English title of one classic in phenomenology of religion is *Religion in Essence and Manifestation,* authored by G. van der Leeuw.[2]

## COMPARATIVE STUDY OF RELIGIONS

Whereas "phenomenology of religion" may be new to you, "comparative religion" is almost certainly not. Most of us are reared in some religious tradition, however tenuously, and we encounter other religions rather early in life. These other religions seize our attention by claiming to be superior to our own religion, or just by being different from it, and so we rather naturally and early find ourselves comparing religions. But whereas "comparing religions" has been going on for thousands of years, "comparative religion," *as an academic field,* was established only in the nineteenth century.[3] Two of the major factors resulting in the establishment of departments of comparative religion were the following: First, there was a great increase in world travel during the nineteenth century. This increase was motivated largely by commercial interests and facilitated greatly by improved means of travel. Such travel took many Europeans and Americans into direct contact for the first time with religions of which they had only heard, and into contact with many more religions of whose existence they had been oblivious. Predictably, these travelers brought back fascinating stories highly embellished by poetic license and misunderstanding! Second, Christian churches took vigorous advantage of these new opportunities to carry out their responsibility to take their message to the ends of the earth (Matt. 28:18). On the one hand, then, there were people who were simply fascinated with these other religions and found themselves telling about them and comparing them. On the other hand, there were missionaries who needed to know in advance something about the indigenous religion(s) of the people to whom they were going. Hence, the missionary enterprise of the nineteenth century created a practical need for the teaching of comparative religions, and it was primarily in response to that need that comparative religion became established in the seminaries and church-related educational institutions of Europe and America.

Motivated by the practical needs of missionaries and operating in a context of Christian commitment, it is understandable that most comparativists (scholars of comparative religion) performed an apologetic as well as an informative function. That is, as well as simply giving students some idea of the number and diversity of religions on earth, the comparativist also endeavored to evaluate these religions in order to show how they stood relative to one another in terms of their various levels of development. This approach to comparative religions was quite in the spirit of the times, considering the dominance then of the evolutionary hypothesis. This hypothesis held that history is a gradual and continual development from lower to higher forms of existence in religion as well as in biology, science, technology, art, and so on. Because part of the widely accepted evolutionary hypothesis was that history moves forward irreversibly and inexorably, comparativists also tried to determine from the past and present the direction in which religious growth was moving. It was assumed that that direction, when grasped clearly and correctly, should be taken as the direction in which we *ought* to move as well as the direction in which history *is* moving inexorably.

Today comparativists have largely dissociated themselves from the assumption that religious progress has moved forward throughout history in a relatively straightforward manner, and that by an examination of history, we can assay the direction in which further religious development should and will take place. This is not to say that comparativists now believe that religions cannot be compared normatively. It means that such comparisons are no longer defended by means of highly abstract, speculative interpretations of history. Rather, it is now widely held that such comparative judgments must be based on an intimate grasp of the details of religions and on a profound grasp of the nature of religion, a grasp that proves its authenticity by being acceptable to religious scholars from diverse religious traditions. In the absence of widely accepted criteria of what is better religiously, comparativists have tended in recent decades to restrict such judgments to developments *within a single tradition*—so that a certain practice in Hinduism, for example, might be judged as an *advance* upon an earlier, similar practice, and, conversely, yet another practice might be judged as a *corruption* of an earlier practice. Such judgments within a single tradition are less controversial than judgments between traditions, but inevitably, I believe, the standards that are clarified for use *within* a tradition will eventually be used to compare traditions to one another. Hence, conceptual progress in the more narrow enterprise will eventually contribute to evaluative discussions in the broader enterprise.

As comparativists today generally dissociate themselves from an uncritical evolutionary approach to religions, they also dissociate themselves from the apologetic task—that is, the task of showing that their own religion is superior to all other religions. There are a number of reasons for this. The most general reason is that whereas an apologetic approach is entirely appropriate in a seminary, which is by its nature devoted to the training of religious professionals in a specific religion, it is entirely inappropriate in a strictly academic context. Hence, (1) as comparativists sought to establish departments of comparative religion in *public* and *nonreligious* institutions of higher education, (2) as persons *without* a religious affiliation became fascinated with the study and teaching of comparative religions, and (3) as comparativists *with* a religious affiliation became interested in practicing their discipline in a *nonapologetic* context, comparativists came to identify their tasks with such things as the following: (a) identifying those themes and elements which cut across and are common to all religions (e.g., ritual, myth, sacrifice, symbolism); (b) showing the diversity of forms which such things as ritual, myth, sacrifice, and symbolism have taken in the world's religions; (c) comparing and contrasting—in an appreciative, nonjudgmental manner—specific religions on these and other common topics; and (d) serving as "brokers" between religious traditions—helping the peoples therein to achieve an accurate and deep understanding of one another, and helping them to find the terms and concepts by means of which they could explain themselves to one another and understand one another. This, in broad terms, seems to be where comparative religion is today—although owing to the recent immense amount of dialogue among scholars and sages from diverse religious traditions, I think the field is also on the verge of establishing widely accepted criteria in terms of which normative discussions can be carried on more freely and vigorously among comparativists from different religious traditions, and between religious and nonreligious scholars. That promises to be an exciting era, and it has already begun to dawn.

## HISTORY OF RELIGIONS

"History of religions" is no doubt a phrase with some immediate meaning for you, given your long acquaintance with the word "history." But today people who use the phrase "history of religions" may mean much more than you think they do. So let's take a look at both the narrower, more familiar meaning and a broader, more recent meaning. In its narrower sense, history of religions is concerned with searching for the origins of each religion (and when this is unavailable, pushing back as far as possible), with tracing its development, and with relating it to the social, political, and economic realities of its cultural context. (This may hardly seem like a "narrow" approach! But I think you'll agree later that it is narrower than the second approach at which we shall look.)

What is the motive for examining a religion in its *historical* context— especially if it claims to be a revelation of God rather than a creation of man? The motive is the assumption that even a revealed religion would *occur* within a specific historical context and would be *conditioned* by that context. It would be cast in the language of a specific people, coined in their metaphors, and aimed at their lives *as they are lived* (and not just in some general abstract sense). In this spirit, Mircea Eliade, distinguished professor of the history of religions, responds to the question, "What can 'history' mean to the student of religion?" "For the student of religion," he writes,

> "history" means primarily that all religious phenomena are conditioned. A *pure* religious phenomenon does not exist. A religious phenomenon is always also a social, an economic, a psychological phenomenon, and, of course, a historical one, because it takes place in historical time and it is conditioned by everything which had happened before.[4]

To say that religious phenomena are *conditioned* by other cultural factors is not to say that they can be explained away in terms of those factors or "reduced" to them. A religious phenomenon is as distinctive as an economic or artistic phenomenon and will never be adequately understood until it is understood as a religious phenomenon. Eliade speaks to this point too:

> To try to grasp the essence of [a religious] phenomenon by means of physiology, psychology, sociology, economics, linguistics, art or any other study is false; it misses the one unique and irreducible element in it—the element of the sacred. Obviously there are no *purely* religious phenomena; no phenomenon can be solely and exclusively religious. Because religion is human it must for that very reason be something social, something linguistic, something economic. . . . . But it would be hopeless to try and explain religion in terms of any one of those basic functions. . . . It would be as futile as thinking you could explain *Madame Bovary* [or any other great novel] by a list of social, economic and political facts. . . .⁵

To expand on this point a bit, the economy of a nation is sometimes influenced by political events; but that doesn't mean that economics is nothing more than an extension of politics. Similarly, religion is sometimes influenced by economic events, but that does not mean that religion is nothing more than a by-product of economic processes. We need to keep these and similar distinctions sharp because they amount to a pragmatic way of mapping out human reality into meaningful, manageable parts of the whole. The interrelationships between these various aspects of human existence—such as politics, philosophy, art, religion, economics, technology, and morality—need to be studied in order that we might understand better their impacts on one another. Nothing seems to be gained and something does seem to be lost whenever we collapse the distinctions between any of these areas or presume to reduce one to another. To be sure, it is not easy to say with precision what religion is, but neither is it easy to say what politics or economics is. These concepts are not the precision instruments we would like them to be, but they do acknowledge the fundamental differences that our experience reveals to us, and we ignore such differences only at the cost of a profound understanding of religion.

We might say, then, that whereas phenomenology of religion is concerned primarily with the methods whereby the meanings, structures, and essences of religious data are apprehended authentically, and whereas the comparativist is devoted to discovering and investigating (concretely as well as abstractly) those themes and elements which are universally characteristic of religions, the primary concern of the historian of religions—in the narrow sense—is to gather, organize, and make a meaningful whole of the concrete data of the entire history of a religion or of some segment thereof. For a good example of the history of religions in this sense, see *The History of Israel* by Martin Noth.

The *broader* meaning of "the history of religions" has developed in the last several decades and is set forth very nicely by Joseph Kitagawa in an article entitled "The History of Religions in America." After pointing out that the phrase "the history of religions" means different things to different people—some thinking of it as "a tour guide" to world religions, others thinking of it as "a historical discipline, analogous to church history," but dealing with many religions, and still others thinking of it as a philosophical search for the universal form of religion that lies beneath all the historical manifestations—Kitagawa writes:

> This apparent ambiguity of the nature of the discipline of the history of religions is reflected in the diversity of names by which it has come to be known, such as comparative religion, phenomenology of religion, science of religions, and history of religions. All these terms, with minor differences, refer to a general body of knowledge known originally as *Allgemeine Religionswissenschaft.* In the English-speaking world the imposing title of "general science of religions" [which is a literal translation of the German phrase in italics] has not been used widely, partly because it is too long and awkward, and partly because the English word "science" tends to be misleading. Thus, the world-wide organization of scholars in this field has recently adopted an official English title, "The International Association for the Study of the History of Religions." It is readily apparent that the term "history of religions" has come to be regarded as a synonym for the "general science of religions," and as such the nature of the discipline must be discussed in the total context of *Religionswissenschaft.* [6]

A number of different phrases in addition to "the general science of religions" have been used by Kitagawa and Eliade to clarify in English the meaning of *Allgemeine Religionswissenschaft*: "the science of religions," "the total science of religions," and "the religio-scientific study of religions." But Kitagawa is correct that any English translation of *Religionswissenschaft* which uses the word "science" stirs up images of physicists, chemists, biologists, and laboratories, whereas in German the term *Wissenschaft* refers not only to the natural sciences and the social sciences, but to *any* field that applies disciplined and rigorous methods of analysis to its subject matter. Hence, in the *Wissenschaft* sense of "science," the disciplines of history and linguistics are sciences, and there can also be a science of religion. But this notion of "science" is foreign to so many Americans and Britishers that it would puzzle and mislead more than it would help. Hence, "the world-wide organization of scholars," to which Kitagawa refers, chose not to use the word "science" in the name by which it now identifies itself.

Clearly, those scholars intended that "the history of religions" should be a more comprehensive study of religions than a history of religions in the narrow sense would be, so let's look at some of the characteristics of the history of religions in its broader, more recent sense. [7] First, the history of religions takes with utmost seriousness the reality and uniqueness of the *experience* of the sacred. Recall, for example, Eliade's statement that it would be folly to try to appreciate *Madame Bovary* entirely in terms of social, economic, and political factors. Similarly, one has not understood a religious phenomenon until one has understood it as a *hierophany*—that is, as a manifestation of the sacred. What is the sacred? Eliade prefers not to make a direct statement in reply to this question, because any attempt to describe the sacred will only diminish or distort our understanding of it. Hence, the best thing to say is simply that it is the opposite of the profane and the secular. Much can be said to make that distinction clear, but what is most effective is not to try to describe the sacred and the profane but to tell stories and give illustrations that bring about in the listener a sense of the difference between the two. Eliade's *The Sacred and the Profane* is devoted to illustrating this difference, and you might take a look also at the first chapter and conclusion of his *Patterns in Comparative Religion.* But the important point here is that whereas the social scientist can legitimately ignore the category of the sacred in many of his analyses of religious behavior, the historian of religions cannot, for, like the phenomenologist and the comparativist, he is trying to understand specific religious phenomena as they are understood by the people for whom they are a revelation of the sacred.

The first point, then, is that the historian of religions finds the unity of his studies in the experiences and embodiments of the sacred found among a people. That is the center from which and to which all his studies move. It is the integrating factor in all that he does as a historian of religions. The second point is that for the historian, the passageway to an accurate and profound understanding of a people's religion is through the unique historical facts which constitute their lives. General impressions based on superficial experience are simply inadequate. Why? Because "every hierophany we look at is also an historical fact. Every manifestation of the sacred takes place in some historical situation."[8] Further, the sacred never manifests itself directly. Rather, it always expresses itself through something other than itself—the wind, the sky, a story, a voice, a stone, a book, a symbol, just about anything! And one's interpretation of these things is inevitably influenced by one's historical context. Further, one should keep in mind that historians of religion have long since given up the idea that "primitive" peoples worshiped these vehicles of the sacred. "It is not the tree, the spring, or the stone that is venerated," Eliade writes, "*but the sacred which is manifested through these cosmic objects.*"[9] The proof of this point is that an object can return to the realm of the profane as well as enter the realm of the sacred. Hence, it is not the object that is worshiped, but the sacred that is manifested through it.

A number of the preceding points are captured nicely in the following passage by Eliade on the Konde people of Tanganyika, Africa:

> The Konde of Tanganyika believe in a Supreme Being, Kyala or Lesa, who, like all the Supreme Beings of the Africans, is endowed with all the majesty of

a heavenly, creating, omnipotent and law-giving God. But Lesa does not only show himself by means of epiphanies of the sky: "Anything great of its kind, such as a great ox or even a great he-goat, or any other impressive object, is called Kyala, by which it may be meant that God takes up his abode temporarily in these things. When a great storm lashes the lake into fury, God is walking on the face of the waters: when the roar of the waterfall is louder than usual, it is the voice of God. The earthquake is caused by his mighty footstep, and the lightning is *lesa,* God coming down in anger. God sometimes comes also in the body of a lion or a snake, and it is in that form that he walks about among men, to behold their doings."[10]

Clearly, we begin to understand the Konde only when we understand what the roar of the waterfall and the stare of the serpent mean to them. Hence, the historian of religion eschews the popular practice of making easy generalizations about other peoples. Instead, he "seeks the basically religious by moving through individual historical religious experiences rather than by ignoring or moving around the peculiar or particular experiences."[11] Such a procedure is slower and more painstaking, but it will almost certainly decrease misunderstandings, misrepresentations, and misappreciations and lead to a much richer, more accurate sense of the nature and significance of the sacred in the lives of a people.

To gain such an understanding of the sacred in other people's lives requires something more than historical methods in the traditional sense. What more is required is, for the most part, precisely what we've talked about already—namely, phenomenology and comparative studies. That combination together with a historical emphasis is largely what the "history of religions" school of thought is all about. Eliade, the main spokesman for this approach, emphasizes that "the history of religions is *not merely a historical discipline,* as, for example, archeology or numismatics. It is equally a *total hermeneutics,* being called to decipher and explicate every kind of encounter of man with the sacred, from prehistory to our day."[12] Clearly, what Eliade is calling for is a comprehensive study of religious meaning that treats the experience of the sacred as unique and central.

We have said so far of the history of religions, in its broader sense, that (1) it takes the sacred seriously, (2) it focuses on the sacred as it is manifested in historical data, and (3) it goes beyond the traditional methods of historians in its efforts to explicate the religion of a people. The final point is that (4) historians of religions believe that their field has valuable cultural contributions to make. Among these are (a) a deeper and more adequate understanding of the nature of man, (b) better communications among people from different religious backgrounds, and—especially important to our own era—(c) an opportunity for people who have lost (or never had) a sense of the sacred, to regain (or gain) an appreciation of what that sense has meant to people in the past and what it might mean to them now. Attractive statements about these cultural values of the history of religions can be found in Eliade's essay, "Crisis and Renewal," in his *The Quest:*

*History and Meaning in Religion,* and in Wilfred Cantwell Smith's paper, "Comparative Religion: Whither—and Why?" in *The History of Religions,* edited by Eliade and Kitagawa (footnotes 4 and 6 at the end of this chapter).

## ANTHROPOLOGY OF RELIGION

This method of approach to religion involves a comprehensive study of religious phenomena in their cultural context. A good example is A. P. Elkin's *The Australian Aborigines: How To Understand Them.* A widely used and comprehensive collection of selections from studies such as Elkin's is the *Reader in Comparative Religion: An Anthropological Approach,* edited by W. A. Lessa and E. Z. Vogt. The methods and data of the anthropologist of religion are very much like those of the historian except that the historian is interested in a broad sweep of time and of cultures, whereas the anthropologist is usually interested in an extant religion as it is now, as an integral part of a culture with its own dynamic tension and unity. Hence, the anthropologist, in order to speak with authority, normally lives among the people whom he (or she) is studying. In this way it is possible to observe directly the place in the lives of the people of their dances, lore, body paint, art work, holy places, and ceremonies. Having focused primarily on primitive peoples who have ways of understanding the world and of living in it that are alien to our European traditions, anthropologists of religion have produced some of the most fascinating literature in modern academia. Consider, for example, Clifford Geertz' description of the ritualization of birth in Java:

> The baby is washed, and then the mother; and there are spells for both of these performances too. The umbilical cord and afterbirth are wrapped in white muslin, put into a jug, salted, and buried outside the house. . . . A little wicker fence is erected around the spot or a broken earthenware pot is inverted over it to keep dogs or other animals from digging it up, and a small candle is kept burning over it for thirty-five days in order to prevent evil spirits from disturbing it.

Geertz continues:

> The burying of the umbilical cord is a serious matter. One woman blamed the death of her child, in convulsion after forty days of life, on the fact that the midwife did not put enough salt in the umbilical cord when she buried it, and so it "came up" and the child died. The cord and afterbirth, coming as it does after the birth of the child, is considered to be his spirit younger brother, while the amniotic fluid which precedes him (it is thrown out up into the air) is considered to be his spirit older brother. For the first thirty-five days they remain near the child and protect him against illness, the first under the ground, the other in the sky.[13]

Regarding the relations of anthropology of religion to history and phenomenology, the present tendency is for the anthropologist to restrict himself to painstaking description of a particular culture and to leave the construction of broad, integrating hypotheses to the historian and the phenomenologist. Clearly, however, the phenomenological *method* is invaluable to the anthropologist as he endeavors to step out of the framework of his own culture so as to see and feel the world as his subjects of study do, and so as to appreciate the religious significance of their behavior, their music, and their creations.

## SOCIOLOGY OF RELIGION

Sociological studies of religion usually take one of two approaches to religion. The one kind we will call the "empirical research approach," and the other we will call the "social construction of reality approach." In some ways, these approaches parallel the "empirical approach" and the "phenomenological approach" of the history of religions, but a comparison of the two is unnecessary at this point. The empirical research approach (ERA, for short) can be broken down into *functional, structural, conflict,* and *significant variable* studies, and even these aren't exhaustive. But a look at each should give you a good idea of the objectives of ERA.

Some sociologists focus on the question, What functions do religious institutions *in fact* serve in society X, and what are the unique functions of religious institutions? The two parts of this question are equally important, for we have discovered in this century—perhaps as never before—that the functions a religious institution serves may not be functions that it alone can serve. Formal education, for example, was handled for centuries by religious institutions. But now they have been largely relieved of that responsibility. Similarly, for centuries churches were the centers of the social life of a community, but now most social life (even for church members) takes place outside of the church. Sociologists want to know why these changes have come about and what impact they are having on religious institutions. Moreover (and this has to do with the second part of the question with which we began), do religious institutions have any social functions of their own which by their very nature cannot be taken away from them? Or are they like the onion which, when all its layers are peeled away, is reduced to nothing because it has no core of its own? If they are not like the onion, then what are the inalienable functions of religious institutions and what role do they play in the functioning of the social whole?

Structural studies, as distinguished from functional studies—though these two are never absolutely separable—focus not on the roles a religion plays in the society of which it is a part but on the various ways the members of that religion structure their environment, their activities, and their relations to one another. In Christianity, for example, the spectrum of social organization ranges from the tight, hierarchical organization of the Roman Catholic Church (which contains several levels of authority culminating in the authority of the pope) to the complete local autonomy of Congregationalist churches, in which decisions are made by democratic processes (the minister having no more authority than any other member of the congregation). Regarding each of these forms of religious organization, the sociologist wants to know not only its structure but also the peculiar problems and the peculiar strengths generated by that structure.

Conflict studies can be sorted into three basic types: (1) conflict within a particular religion, (2) conflict between different religions, and (3) conflict between religious and nonreligious institutions such as the state. Such studies, it should be noted, have a "dialectical" angle. That is, it is assumed that change comes about by means of the interaction of institutions, and that religious institutions are not merely products of social processes but are causes of changes in those processes. The influence of nonreligious institutions on religious institutions is not unidirectional. The influence is reciprocal, and so sociologists examine the ways in which religious and nonreligious institutions modify one another. To give some examples of these various types of conflict beginning with (1) above, structuralist studies lead naturally into an examination of the conflicts that seem to be generated by the very nature of the organization of a particular religious group. The Episcopal Church, for example, does not at this time permit ordination of women to the priesthood. But "women's equality" is a vibrant cause these days, and Episcopal women are fighting for the right to ordination. Moreover, I shall not be surprised if they have achieved their aim before this book goes to press. I shall be surprised, however, if sociologists do not present us with a "micro"-level study of the people and factors involved in this struggle for women's ordination.

Conflict *between* different religions is a matter of everyday news and has long been under investigation by sociologists. Catholics and Protestants fight in Northern Ireland, as do Jews and Muslims in Palestine and Hindus and Muslims in India. But to what extent are these *really* religious battles? And to what extent are the names "Protestant" and "Catholic" merely convenient labels with which to differentiate groups who only happen to be Catholic and Protestant but who are really fighting over economic or other matters? And to what extent, sociologists will ask, are the religions involved and their leadership serving to mitigate or exacerbate the conflict?

Third, sociologists investigate relations between religion and the state. The history of conflicts between religion and state in the United States is particularly interesting because European conflict between church and state helped populate America; yet the U.S.A. has hardly provided unrestricted religious liberty for its citizens. In the nineteenth century the Mormons were persecuted for practicing polygamy (though it was approved by their own religious laws), and in this century Amish children in Wisconsin have been required by state law to go to a state-accredited school through the tenth grade—in spite of the fact that Amish adults insisted that formal schooling beyond the eighth grade was irrelevant to the rustic style of life to which they were religiously committed. (The Amish won their case in court only recently.) Outside this country, newspapers and magazines (even as I write this paragraph) tell of Russian oppression of its Jewish citizens (and, indeed, of all its religious citizens, since Marxist communism is militantly atheistic), and of African persecution of black Jehovah's Witnesses (who believe in strict political neutrality, and who are, therefore, a thorn in the side of those nationalistic leaders who want every citizen to acclaim their policies). The attacks haven't all been from the side of the state, of course. Mahatma Gandhi, a Hindu religious leader, helped India fight for its political independence from Great Britain, and religious groups in the U.S.A. have fought in behalf of racial justice and women's rights.

Perhaps I should add as a counterbalance that sociologists are interested also in the ways in which state and religion bolster one another. Sometimes religion is co-opted by the state and vice versa because it behooves a state to be able to declare divine authority for its earthly policies and because it behooves a religion to have the earthly power to implement its God-given mandate. In addition to the cooperative relations between highly visible religious institutions (such as Methodism) and the state, sociologists are also interested in what has come to be known as "civil religion"—a kind of distillation of elements from the spirit of nationalism and the mainline religions. Apparently civil religion is often more important to the citizens of a nation than the mainline religions to which they belong! Andrew Greeley calls civil religion the "super religion" (that is, the religion *above* the more obvious religions), while Will Herberg, thinking of his own nation, calls civil religion "the religion of Americanism." For a brief introduction to this fascinating phenomenon, see Chapter 7, "The Civil Religion," in Greeley's *The Denominational Society* (refer to bibliography at the end).

Finally, what I have called "significant variable studies" are efforts by sociologists to discover the cause-effect relationships of which religious phenomena are a part. It is a rather well-known fact, for example, that the denomination to which a protestant Christian belongs can be guessed with a good degree of accuracy if you know the individual's socioeconomic status. But socioeconomic status is only one variable that can be linked up with religious facts. John Photiadis and B. B. Maurer, in a research project titled "Religion in an Appalachian State," took four religious variables—(1) intensity of religious beliefs; (2) need to use religion as a buffer from the outside world; (3) preference of a religious way of life; and (4) degree of church participation—and conducted research in order to see how these items correlated with fluctuations in the following kinds of nonreligious variables: age, family size, socioeconomic status, perception of one's own health, social alienation, and type of job. The correlations found were sometimes what you would expect, but not always. As would be expected, there was a larger percentage of "strong believers" among those who considered themselves to be ill than among those who considered themselves to be healthy, but the degree of church participation tended to *decrease* as intensity of religious belief *increased*![14] Sociologists are also interested in determining the extent to which religious institutions are *creators* and *critics* of society and the extent to which they are *products* of secular forces. For example, to what extent have religious institutions made significant contributions to the quest for racial justice in the United States, and to what extent have they been, in the words of Martin Luther King, Jr., "taillights instead of headlights"? Also, regarding prejudice, do religious people tend to be more or less prejudiced than nonreligious people? And how does prejudice vary among religious groups? Is it true, as some wit put it, that "11 A.M. on Sunday is the most segregated hour of the week"? Do more religious persons than secular persons contribute to benevolent causes and involve themselves in social movements for justice? or is it the other way around? or are the two groups indistinguishable with regard to these questions?

The striking results of one sociological investigation were reported by the *National Health Federation Bulletin* in October of 1971. It reads as follows:

> Dr. George Comstock of Johns Hopkins University recently conducted exhaustive tests on 567 men. The results proved that men who attended church regularly stood twice the chance of avoiding fatal heart attacks, cancer, tuberculosis, chronic bronchitis, suicidal tendency and cirrhosis of the liver.

The report goes on to say:

> NHF does not involve itself in religion, but this test, which was investigated by us, is so conclusive that we are reporting it. Apparently the psychic or emotional response to a religious oriented life in church relieves stresses that otherwise have a deleterious physiological effect on our bodies. An original survey on which the study was based included 91,000 persons.

We need more studies of this kind, and of the other empirical kinds, in spite of the fact that they may be embarrassing to religious institutions as often as they are flattering. After all, if we don't have the facts, we can neither criticize nor praise religion justly.

You should now have a good grasp of the kinds of questions that are investigated by sociologists who are oriented to the empirical research approach, so let's take a brief look at the "social construction of reality approach" (SCR, for short). Philip Hauser points out that sociology is a specialized social science which is distinguished from the other social sciences by a basic fact with which it starts and a basic assumption which underlies its investigations. "The basic fact is the relative helplessness of the human infant at birth who is always born into, and depends for his survival upon, a social group. The fundamental assumption is that the conduct of the person—his ways of thinking and ways of acting—and the nature of the social order—its structure, function, and values—are to be understood as a product of group life."[15] It is this "fundamental assumption" which provides the key to SCR. It is, to be sure, a "methodological assumption," —that is, a working hypothesis rather than something one must believe to be true. But the fact it is a working hypothesis rather than a certitude in no way relieves the sociologist from his or her responsibility *as* a sociologist to see if all human behavior cannot be explained adequately according to this assumption.

The point of this assumption is quite radical, compared to our ordinary ways of thinking, for ordinarily we attribute a good deal of an individual's behavior to his "free" choices, or we say, "That's just the way she is." But look at that fundamental methodological assumption again (hereafter, FMA). It says that not only an individual's ways of acting but also his ways of thinking are generated from the interaction between him and his social context. This is a claim we accept easily when we limit it to common ways of behaving, such as shaking hands, and common ways of thinking, such as arithmetic and certain historical facts. But the point of FMA is much more radical than that. It is claiming that even what we do in our deepest moments of solitude is a product of the interaction between ourselves and our social environment (and remember, all we are at birth is an unconditioned organism—all the conditioning comes from our natural and social environments, not from ourselves). I must admit that I am sometimes startled at how profoundly a child embodies the gait, the posture, and the gestures of a parent. At times it is sufficiently eerie that I begin to realize the extent to which not only his gait, posture, and gestures, but also his values, moods, beliefs, and ways of perceiving and feeling the world have been *instilled into/absorbed by* him from his social environment, unwittingly.

The sociologist of religion who takes the SCR approach is profoundly interested in the socialization processes whereby a particular interpretation of reality—e.g., the Christian interpretation—*becomes reality to the individual,* usually a child. As Berger and Luckmann put it in their *The Social Construction of Reality,* "The child does not internalize the world of his significant others as one of many possible worlds. He internalizes it as *the* world, the only existent and only conceivable world, the world *tout court.*"[16] To the child the world is the way it is interpreted to him by his significant others—that is, the adults who are most important to him. That is his natural way of seeing the world. Hence, that particular *interpretation* of reality *is* reality to him—and not only to him or to her but to all of us as children. To repeat, the SCR sociologist wants to understand better the social processes by means of which a particular interpretation of reality becomes reality to the child. He wants to understand the social genesis of religious attitudes, behaviors, and belief systems. He wants to know what means (e.g., myths, rituals, symbols, behavior patterns) a religion uses to maintain its sense of reality in the everyday lives of its members. And how does it cope with the lure of other religions in a pluralistic society or with the doubts about religion that are engendered in a secularized society? How does it legitimate its own belief system and "illegitimate" that of others? What stratagems does it use to bring deviants back into line and to make other symbolic universes (interpretations of reality) appear unreal or unattractive? These kinds of questions and this approach are associated especially with the work of Peter Berger and Thomas Luckmann. See the *Social Construction of Reality* for the theoretical foundation of their individual works on sociology of religion such as Berger's *The Sacred Canopy* and Luckmann's *The Invisible Religion* (refer to bibliography at the end).

## PSYCHOLOGY OF RELIGION

Psychologists of religion are especially interested in the effects that different religious beliefs and practices have on the integration and disintegration of personality. Do more theists or atheists experience mental breakdowns? Do more Protestants or Catholics commit suicide? More fundamentally, is the fullest development of personality possible apart from some kind of religious faith? One eminent psychiatrist, Carl Jung, reports in *Modern Man in Search of a Soul* that his extensive practice as a psychiatrist led him to the insight that all of his patients over thirty-five were ill because they had lost their religious understanding of the world and they recovered their mental health only when they recovered that outlook. Such a claim by such an eminent psychiatrist cannot be overlooked. Yet neither can we overlook the contention of Sigmund Freud, founder of psychoanalysis and one of the most influential thinkers of our century, that religion is a form of neurotic immaturity (see his *The Future of an Illusion*). Clearly, whoever is right, Freud or Jung, about the impact of religion on personal development and maturation, this is a question that must be submitted to critical inquiry and not left to mere prejudice and opinion. Hence the need for the investigation of religion by psychologists.

Please keep in mind, however, that the psychologist of religion is not concerned to say "good" or "bad" about religious beliefs and  practices.

As a scientist, he or she is concerned only to clarify the *consequences* for personality of being religious in a certain way or of being religious at all. Value judgments such as "good" and "bad," "right" and "wrong," "ought" and "ought not" do not fall within the province of the scientist as scientist. This is true for the sociologist, the anthropologist, and the historian, as well as for the psychologist. Neither do these persons in their capacities as social scientists normally ask about the truth or falsity of the religion they are investigating. Their limited but important objective is to *understand and describe.* This is, nonetheless, a crucial task because until the facts about a religion are known, we can evaluate it neither fairly nor accurately. We can only make flights of rhetoric. In conclusion, scientific studies of religion can be intrinsically interesting and are instrumentally important to intelligent decision making.

"But surely," you must be asking by now, "*some* discipline must engage primarily in the task of *evaluating* religions?" That task, I believe, belongs in a sense to each and every person, for it involves decisions that are much too personal for us to leave to others. Still, there is a discipline that facilitates the making of intelligent decisions about the truth of religious claims—namely, philosophy of religion.


## PHILOSOPHY OF RELIGION

Whereas the social scientists use their methods of research to discover *what* people do and believe of a religious nature, philosophers of religion use philosophical methods of inquiry to try to ascertain the *truth or falsity* of people's religious beliefs and the *morality or immorality* of their codes of behavior. Philosophers of religion sometimes go further and ask more radical questions such as: Does the idea of an absolute right and wrong make sense? (That is, if standards of right and wrong are based on human opinions, and if human opinions vary and change how can there be an absolute right and wrong?) And what does God have to do with what is morally right and wrong? (Isn't what is morally right independent of the will of God? What if God had commanded us to torture infants?) Moreover, does the idea of God even make sense? (We know what we mean when we talk about sticks and stones, animals and people, or even stars and planets, but what in the world can be meant by "God" if God is "an infinite, incorporeal spirit," as He is often said to be?) Also, is life after death even conceivable, much less possible? (Isn't it the case that when my body disintegrates, I lose my personal identity forever? How can it make sense to talk about me surviving the death of my body? How could a disembodied me be anything at all?)[17]

Clearly, philosophy of religion is a highly intellectual approach to religion. It wants to know whether a religious claim is meaningful (that is, makes sense), and if so, what kind of meaning it has, and what its meaning is, and whether it is true or false, and how its truth or falsity might be demonstrated. Such an approach to religion is as unavoidable as it is inadequate. It is inadequate because there is always far more to religious faith, as we shall see, than believing intellectually that certain propositions are true; yet, it is an unavoidable approach because none of us wants to believe that which is demonstrably false or wrong. We want to believe that which is true, or, if we can't establish what is *true,* we want to believe that which is most *probably true,* or, if we can't establish even that, we want at least to believe that which is *possibly true*! Hence, we inevitably become involved in questions of truth and falsity, probability and improbability, possibility and impossibility. And that is largely what philosophical inquiry is about.

## THEOLOGY

Theology differs from philosophy of religion in that whereas philosophy of religion involves no initial assumptions about the truth or falsity of a particular religious doctrine or the morality or immorality of a particular religious code, theology *begins* with the affirmation of certain religious codes and doctrines and works forward from these. This is not to say that all theologians believe they *know* that the claims of their religion are true. Some would go this far, but others would say only that they believe the evidence shows that their religion is the one which is *most likely* true. Still others would make the even weaker claim that they have a profound but nonrational *feeling* that their religion is true; and still others would say that they only *hope* that their religion is true. We shall look more closely at each of these four attitudes in Chapter 6. For now it is important only to realize that when the theologian affirms a religious doctrine or code, he is not necessarily claiming that he knows that it is true. Hence, when reading a theologian, it is important to discover not only *what* he affirms but also the attitude of his affirmation. Still, the primary work of the theologian as theologian lies not in what he affirms, for he very likely shares his religious affirmations with many people who are not theologians, at least in any professional sense; e.g., a Catholic theologian shares his affirmation of the Apostles' Creed with millions of lay Catholics. Rather, his work as a theologian is primarily a matter of (1) *clarifying* in contemporary terms the meaning of that which he affirms (such as the Buddhist idea of reincarnation), (2) *working out the theoretical implications* of his beliefs (by this process understanding becomes deeper and more detailed, and sometimes new doctrines are deduced, such as the Catholic doctrine of the Immaculate Conception), and (3) *working out the practical applications* of his faith to the contemporary social scene (Mahatma Gandhi rejected the ancient class of "untouchables" on the grounds that it was contrary to the spirit of

Hindu sacred literature). Clearly, the theologian works *within* a religious tradition and is a servant *of* it, whereas a philosopher, as philosopher, stands *outside* a religious tradition and directs his questions *to* it. If I might brandish my infamous broad brush again, whereas the preacher (whose task is closely related to that of the theologian) *declares* a proposition and calls for *commitment* to it, the philosopher *analyzes* that same proposition and calls for *justification* of it. Personally, I do not see these two roles as antithetical but as the positive and negative poles between which the human spirit most oscillate in its search for that which is most worthy of commitment.

In view of the fact that I sometimes get from people the attitude that the philosopher is more honest than the theologian, since the philosopher hasn't "sold out" to some particular doctrine, I must add the following. There is nothing wrong with finding yourself committed to a belief and then trying to understand more fully its significance and implications. This is essentially what the theologian does, and I don't see how intellectual progress can be made except in this manner. Further, the philosopher *does* have his own presuppositions when he investigates religious beliefs; it's just that they aren't about religious doctrines—more likely they are about logic, language, and the nature of knowledge.[18] Without such presuppositions, the philosopher would be able to do nothing since he would have no standards by which to make judgments; yet few, if any, philosophers these days claim that their presuppositions are demonstrably true. Hence, philosophers, too, are operating on the basis of presuppositions that are debatable. Yet neither the philosopher nor the theologian has "sold out." Both are simply proceeding according to the best that they know in their respective areas of inquiry.

Finally, it should be noted that *the same person can be both theologian and philosopher.* To be sure, in order to do theology a person must have a religious faith on which to reflect, but one can have such a faith without blinding oneself to the philosophical questions that can be put to that faith and to religious faith in general. Being aware of such questions, a person can choose to attempt to answer them, and when he does so, he is doing philosophy. He must be careful, of course, not to let his faith interfere with the integrity and the intensity of his philosophical investigations. Finally, even as the professional theologian may raise philosophical questions about his faith, the professional philosopher is not prevented by his vocation from having a religious faith. As a person who must act on the basis of probability and hope or else perish, the philosopher need not, any more than any other person, allow the legitimate philosophical ideal of perfect and certain knowledge to impoverish his inner life and paralyze his ability to act. If we require 100 percent certainty before carrying on our daily lives, we will never move! And when we do move on probabilities, we don't move only 60 percent of ourselves because the probability of success is only 60 percent! We take 100 percent of ourselves into action—

whether the odds are high or low, with us or against us. We cannot do otherwise. Whence some of the anguish of life.

## EXISTENTIALISM

Finally, I call your attention to the existentialist approach to religion. This approach is not as completely cerebral as philosophy of religion nor as impersonal as social science studies of religion. It is at one and the same time *emotional and intellectual, subjective and objective.* It is an approach in which you are deeply and personally concerned about yourself, about reality, and about your relation to it. A shift of perspective moves you from asking, What is man? to asking, Who am I? from asking, What is our duty as persons? to asking, What ought I to do in this situation? from asking, What is death? to asking, Why am I dying? Both types of question are legitimate and important, but to ask the second kind of question is, it seems to me, an inevitable moment in the process of religious study, for at some point you will pass from the disinterested question, What do those people believe and do of a religious nature? to the personal and passionate question, What do their beliefs and practices have to do with my existence? A Catholic priest I once met was aware of this possible switch from being disinterested to being interested so that when I took a group of students to visit his monastery for a weekend (we had also visited Jewish, Unitarian, and Hindu groups), the first thing that the priest did was to take the students aside and impress upon them that though they might be coming with a purely academic attitude, three days in such an atmosphere might precipitate some very genuine personal struggles. He did not want them to be caught unawares by such an event lest they think that it had somehow been engineered. Such alterations in perception can be engineered of course but they needn't be, for sometimes what we approach initially out of sheer curiosity we soon find ourselves very personally involved in. Perhaps I should issue a similar warning, for the remainder of this book is not a disinterested academic analysis of religion. Rather, it is an attempt to convey what religion has meant and can mean to human beings at its best. Hence, it is the existential approach we will be taking throughout the remainder of our time together, but with considerable doses of phenomenology of religion (regarding the essence of religion), philosophy of religion (regarding the essence of belief and faith), and psychology of religion (regarding religion and personal development). For those of you who are interested in the other approaches mentioned, such as history of religions, anthropology of religion, sociology of religion, comparative religion, and theology, there are separate sections included in the bibliography at the end of the book. (For books on *theology,* see the section titled "Theism." Parenthetically, it's a great bibliography, so I hope you'll do some browsing in it soon! In fact, it might be a good "change of pace" before beginning the next chapter.)

## Footnotes

1. Wilfred Cantwell Smith, *The Faith of Other Men* (New York: Mentor Books, 1965), p. 40.

2. Gerardus van der Leeuw, *Religion in Essence and Manifestation* (New York: Harper & Row, Publishers, 1963).

3. See the brief "Chronological Survey" of the study of religions at the end of Mircea Eliade's *The Sacred and the Profane* (New York: Harcourt, Brace & World, Inc., 1959).

4. Mircea Eliade, *The Quest: History and Meaning in Religion* (Chicago: The University of Chicago Press, 1969), p. 52.

5. Mircea Eliade, *Patterns in Comparative Religion* (New York: The New American Library, Inc., 1958), p. xiii.

6. In Mircea Eliade and Joseph Kitagawa, eds., *The History of Religions* (Chicago: The University of Chicago Press, 1959), p. 15.

7. Henceforth when I use the phrase "history of religions," I will be using it in its broader sense, unless noted otherwise.

8. Eliade, *Patterns in Comparative Religion,* p. 2.

9. Eliade, *The Quest,* p. 52.

10. Eliade, *Patterns in Comparative Religion,* p. 27.

11. Eliade and Kitagawa, *The History of Religions,* p. viii.

12. Eliade, *The Quest,* p. 58. Italics mine.

13. Quoted from *The Religion of Java* by Clifford Geertz, in Michael Pye, *Comparative Religion* (New York: Harper & Row, Publishers, 1972), pp. 63–64.

14. See "Religion in an Appalachian State," by John Photiadis and B. B. Maurer, Appalachian Center, Research Report 6, West Virginia University, February 1974.

15. See "Sociology," by Philip M. Hauser, *Encyclopaedia Britannica* (1970), 20, 784.

16. Peter L. Berger and Thomas Luckmann, *The Social Construction of Reality* (Garden City, N.Y.: Doubleday & Company, Inc., 1966), p. 124.

17. D. Z. Phillips in *Death and Immortality* (New York: St. Martin's Press, 1970), argues the inconceivability and therefore the impossibility of survival of death. H. D. Lewis in *The Self and Immortality* (New York: Seabury Press, Inc., 1973), argues that survival of death is conceivable and is therefore possible.

18. See, for example, the kinds of philosophical tools that are developed in Wesley Salmon's *Logic,* 2nd ed., 1973, William Alston's *Philosophy of Language,* 1964, and Roderick Chisholm's *Theory of Knowledge,* 1966, all published in Prentice-Hall's Foundations of Philosophy Series.

# Interpretations of Religion

QUESTIONS TO THINK ABOUT

- What does it mean to be "religiously concerned"?
- What does it mean "to have a religious faith"?
- What shall we mean by the word "God"?
- What shall we mean by the word "deity"?
- What shall we mean by the word "Lord"?
- What is idolatry?
- What is Erich Fromm's definition of religion?
- What important factor does Fromm omit from his definition?
- What is pseudo-religion?
- What is crypto-religion?
- What are the characteristics of authentic religion?
- What is meant by saying that "reality is ambiguous"?
- Why do I say the question is not *whether* to be religious but *how* to be religious? Do you agree with me?
- Do you agree that there are assumptions about reality and value presently operative in your attitudes and actions?
- What are those assumptions?

## A METHODOLOGICAL PRELUDE

In this chapter and the chapters that follow, I will be setting forth an understanding of religion which I hope will prove provocative and valuable. But as I proceed, please keep in mind that I am not presuming to tell you what religion "really is." The very idea of saying what something really is involves philosophical problems that could easily sidetrack us for many many pages. Indeed, one can spend a lifetime on these problems, normally dealt with in philosophy in the subareas of *epistemology* (theory of knowledge) and *metaphysics* (theory of reality). I shall not be presuming, then, to tell you what religion is in some complete and final sense; yet neither do I believe that my understanding of religion is completely arbitrary. I think I am hitting the target—though perhaps not in the bull's-eye. I am trying to account for certain data in human experience and believe I am succeeding to some extent. So I hope you will take seriously what I have to say. However, I also hope that you will continuously ask yourself how well my ideas fit your own experience and thinking, for these may bring you to believe that my understanding of religion is *inadequate* and therefore needs to be supplemented, or is plain *wrong* and needs to be corrected. Hence, I invite your reactions. Fill the margins! It is only by acknowledging and clarifying our disagreements that we can discuss them honestly and fully, and it is only by rigorous dialogue that we shall make rapid progress toward a more adequate and convincing understanding of religion than either of us has now.

My method of procedure in setting forth that interpretation of religion which I find exciting and authentic will be to develop a set of terms by means of which we can better understand ourselves and others regarding religious matters. These terms will then serve as tools with which we can analyze religious phenomena and thereby understand better their structure and dynamics. My exposition of these terms, such as "God" and "faith," has been greatly influenced by the work of Professor Paul Tillich, but I have not attempted to restrict myself to Tillich's conclusions. Readers who are interested in Tillich's position are encouraged to read first his outstanding little volume, *Dynamics of Faith* (refer to bibliography at the end).

## RELIGIOUS CONCERN

Earlier we spoke of a person "awakening religiously," of a seed of religious concern germinating. But what does it mean to awaken religiously, to be religiously concerned? It means that a person is gripped by the question, What is *ultimately* real and valuable? There are many versions and variants of this question, but they always have to do with *the individual's existence in relation to reality.* These are never impersonal questions. They are always impassioned. They have to do with *my* origins, *my* destiny, all considered in a cosmic context. What is the nature of the reality within which I live and breathe and have my being? What is the nature of my existence within that reality? What within that reality, if anything, is sacred—that is, gives absolute meaning, worth, unity, richness, and exaltation to human life, and therefore to my life?

Now if "to be religious" means in its simplest sense "to be religiously concerned," then every normal person is potentially religious, for every normal person is capable of being haunted by the question, What is ultimate? Indeed, I think that a person cannot become fully human until he or she has confronted the question of ultimates and begun the religious quest. Moreover, the circumstances of our lives push us in the direction of raising the religious question, so that whether or not reality includes an encouraging answer, it does constrain us to raise the question. (Later we will examine some of the conditions of our existence which contribute to the germination of the seeds of religious concern.) Hence, the *academic study* of religion may be only for academic types, but religion itself, concern for that which is ultimate, touches every human being. As John Magee, an admirer of Tillich's, puts it,

> whenever a human being [1] speaks of the ultimate meaning of his existence, [2] considers his absolute obligations, or [3] relates himself by commitment or devotion to what he thinks is ultimately real—whenever he does any of these things, he is acting religiously, whether he realizes it or not.[1]

## RELIGIOUS FAITH: GOD, DEITY, AND THE LORD

Whereas *to be religiously concerned* is to be concerned about what is ultimate, *to have a religious faith* is to feel that you have found that which is ultimately real and valuable (or that it has revealed itself to you).[2] Note that both states, concern and faith, are characterized by duality: there is a Subject (you) who is passionately concerned and an Object of that concern. Prior to faith, the concern of the Subject is to *discover* that which is ultimately real and valuable. After faith has emerged, the concern of the Subject is to *sustain* his relationship to the Object which he has experienced as sacred, as worthy of worship, of absolute commitment and devotion. Such faith may be dynamic, for the individual may seek an ever deeper understanding of the object of his faith, and, if experience proves the object of his faith to be deficient, he may seek an ever more adequate object of faith.

Tillich suggests that this object of religious commitment should be called "God"—no matter what it is. In other words, the word "God" should be applied to whatever fulfills the *function* of giving to an individual the conviction that it is that which is ultimately real and valuable. That thing does, in fact, function as God (as the absolute) in that person's life. Now this might seem an odd, even blasphemous, use of the term "God," but it is really quite biblical. Consider, for example, a story about the ancient Israelite prophet, Elijah. Disturbed by the defection of many Israelites to the worship of the Canaanite deity Baal, Elijah decided it was time to have a showdown with the worshippers of Baal. Elijah successfully challenged the priests of Baal to meet him on top of Mount Carmel in order that the true God might be revealed. When all were gathered he declared, "If Baal is God, then we should worship Baal; but if the Lord is God, then we should worship the Lord." Clearly, Elijah did not beg the question as to who was the true God, Baal or the Lord. He simply raised the question in a pointed way, using the word "God" to refer to that which *is* worthy of our worship, of our absolute trust and commitment. He left the resolution of the question to the events of the day. The progress of the confrontation is fascinating indeed, Elijah proving to be a sharp-tongued wit. If you haven't read the book or seen the movie, I invite you to put down this book and turn to the eighteenth chapter of the book of I Kings in the Bible—but hurry back.

Tillich is correct to insist on the importance of having functional interpretations of religious terms, since such interpretations enable us to see more clearly how religion cuts across and finds expression in all societies and all lives. Still, it is not enough to define just one term, "God," in this manner, for that term gains clarity only over against other terms. Hence, let's define "God," "deity," and "Lord," and see if the definitions of any two of these words do not help make more clear the meaning of the third word. We shall use the word "God" to stand for that which *is* worthy of our ultimate concern and commitment because it is ultimately real and valuable. The word "deity" we shall use to refer to that which a person *treats as though* it is worthy of absolute commitment (whether it really is or not). A person's deity is that which actually dominates that person's life, giving it unity, direction, and inspiration, whether the person realizes what it is or not. Karl Jaspers, a twentieth-century German psychiatrist and philosopher, put this point nicely when he stated, "That which you hold to, upon which you stake your existence, that is truly your God" (though we would now substitute "deity" where he has said "God"). Jaspers goes on to make another point which shall be assumed throughout this book: "Man cannot help taking something as an absolute, whether willingly and knowingly, whether accidentally and fitfully or resolutely and steadfastly. Man has a kind of home in the absolute. He cannot evade it. In that home he must live."[3] (We shall return shortly to the phenomenon of a person being unaware of that which dominates his life.) Owing to the nature of its usage in English translations of the Bible, we shall reserve our third term, "the Lord," for reference to the deity of Jews and Christians.[4]

Many things other than the Lord have been deities, of course. One of these alternatives was captured in a felicitous expression by a student who said that some people are "very religious about money"! Consider, for example, the experience of my brother, Daniel, who drove a man a couple of hundred miles because the fellow was down on his luck and needed a break. When they arrived at their destination the man, whom my brother knew, handed him some money. My brother refused it and said, "I drove you because I'm your friend." The fellow dropped the money on his lap and said, "That's the only friend you'll ever have." And what about the Great Depression of the thirties? People committed suicide because their wealth was wiped out. It was as though they were saying, "God is dead, so I may as well be too." Other prominent deities for which persons have lived and died include sex, fame, power, pleasure, security, success, the nation, justice, love, peace, self, and humanity. If you put your mind to it, you can think of still others. As Radhakrishnan, a Hindu thinker, has put it, "The age of faith is always with us; only the object of our faith changes."[5]

## IDOLATRY

Inasmuch as there are many possible objects of religious faith, we must ask, Are all of these objects *equally* worthy of our commitment, or are some more worthy than others? Most important, *is* there anything that is worthy of our *absolute* commitment and devotion? Is there anything that is truly worthy of *worship?* Kai Nielsen focused the problem sharply when he stated, "The religious quest is a quest to find a Z such that Z is worthy of worship."[6] My own position is that some objects are more worthy of devotion than others: For example, self-fulfillment should be valued over self-indulgence and the welfare of humanity over the supremacy of one's nation. Is not your own conviction that some things are more worthy of commitment than others? Now since the objects to which we can commit ourselves are many in number, and since they are not equally worthy of our commitment, we are faced with the problems of (1) deciding among them and (2) avoiding *idolatry.* What is idolatry? In its extreme form, it consists of *giving unconditional devotion to something that is not worthy of such devotion*—such things as money or winning or one's nation. From another angle we might say that idolatry consists of giving more of yourself to something or someone than it or that person deserves. The greater the discrepancy between the intensity of your devotion and the worth of the object of your devotion, the greater the idolatry.

If Tillich is correct that everyone is religious in the sense of having an ultimate concern, then that includes you and me, and we each need to ask ourselves what our deity *is* and whether it is an object worthy of our absolute commitment or an idol—i.e., something which is *not able to deliver* what we expect of it, something which will *disillusion* us, something the deficiencies of which we *must blind ourselves* to in order that we can remain committed to it. Is our deity God or an idol? Which deity is God? And how do we avoid idolatry? Karl Jaspers, in his *Way to Wisdom*, makes the interesting suggestion that idolatry results from mistaking for God that which only *points* to God. Instead of responding to the pointer—e.g., political power—by transcending to God, we fixate on the pointer by becoming obsessed with it, as though there were nothing more important or greater. But the pointer, whether it be power, fame, ecstasy, or something else, is no more the same as God than a finger that points at the moon is the moon. Most of us have been amused and frustrated by our attempts to point something out to a baby. All the baby cares to look at is the finger that keeps punctuating the air with its pointing! Perhaps in more difficult matters we adults are still susceptible to mistaking the finger for the moon, the pointer for the referent.[7]

**F RANKLY SPEAKING**                                    **by Phil Frank**

'DON'T DISTURB YOUR FATHER WHILE HE'S PRAYING!'

## THE NATURE OF RELIGION: ERICH FROMM

Now I would like to begin again by setting forth a second analysis of religion—not because it contradicts the earlier analysis, but because it is so similar. What *is* different is the background of the author, Erich Fromm. It seems significant to me that Tillich, a believer in the biblical God (see his difficult but valuable lectures, *Biblical Religion and the Search for Ultimate Reality),*[8] and Fromm, who rejects the biblical God (see his *Psychoanalysis and Religion*),[9] arrive at such similar conclusions about religion. People starting from such different perspectives and arriving at such similar conclusions must be on to something! Fromm, a practicing psychoanalyst and author of such popular books as *The Art of Loving* and *Revolution of Hope,* does not believe that the Lord is God but believes nonetheless that religion is something humanly important. He states in *Psychoanalysis and Religion* that by the word "religion" he understands, "any system of thought and action shared by a group which gives to the individual a frame of orientation and an object of devotion."[10] He goes on to claim that a human being (in the biological sense) cannot become a person without a frame of orientation and an object of devotion. Why? Because to be human is a merely biological matter, whereas to be a person requires a certain level of development, of awareness, sensitivity, and commitment. Without these things we fall short of human fulfillment and may even perish, owing to our lack of any instinctual frame of orientation or object of commitment. Hence, John Magee, author of *Religion and Modern Man,* says that religion is "life orientation, a [person's] mode of getting his bearings in the world."[11] The question then is never *whether* to be religious—we must be in order to be fully human; the question is *how* to be religious. Again we are confronted with the *opportunity* and *necessity* of choice, for the religions and philosophies of the world confront us precisely as different ways to be religious.

Before going on, let's analyze briefly two deficiencies of Fromm's otherwise fine definition. First, Fromm has focused on two of the central concerns of religion—i.e., the nature of reality and what is of genuine worth—but he has neglected a third and equally important concern—namely, the concern for rebirth, for transformation, for an extraordinary inner source of strength and peace and guidance and joy. In biblical terminology, Fromm has provided for the Father (the Genesis frame of orientation accepted by Jews and Christians holds that the Lord created the heavens and the earth and is the ruler of history), and for the Torah/Son (Jews are devoted to study of and obedience to the commandments of the Torah—i.e., the first five books of the *Bible*—and Christians are devoted to a person, Jesus, whom they believe to be the only Son of God), but Fromm has not provided for the Holy Spirit, which is described by Jews and Christians alike as their source of strength, joy, and transformation. To be sure, the devotion of Jews to the commandments of the Torah is of a different nature than the devotion of Christians to Jesus, and their interpretations of the Holy Spirit also differ significantly. I do not mean to deny these differences, but only to point up the functional similarity between three central foci of the religious faith of Jews and Christians. Moreover, I think these three elements—frame of orientation (a matter of the mind), object or devotion (a matter of the will), and source of transformation (a matter of the heart)—are central to any fully developed religion.

There are, of course, religions that are (1) almost completely moralistic, emphasizing the object of devotion to the neglect of the frame of orientation and the source of transformation; and there are religions that are (2) almost completely Pentecostal or Dionysian, emphasizing the source of transformation to the neglect of the other two elements of a fully developed religion; and there are religions that are (3) primarily a matter of the intellect, focusing on a particular understanding of the world without much regard for the inner life or the life of action. When we put two of these elements together without the third, we get combinations that sound familiar: (a) an emphasis on reason and morality with a neglect of the spirit, (b) an emphasis on morality and spirit with a neglect of reason, or (c) an emphasis on reason and spirit, with a neglect of morality. But no two of these factors by themselves, it seems to me, can provide what the human spirit is seeking in religion. In our religion we want to acquire a way of understanding the world, a sense of what is really valuable, and a source of spiritual sustenance. Anything less is not enough. Perhaps that is why we see an increasing interest in mysticism among liberal religious groups, and an increasing involvement in social action by Pentecostal groups. The very nature of our existence makes us discontented with anything less than a fully developed religion.

The second debatable aspect of Fromm's definition of religion is his claim that religion is, and presumably must be, "shared by a group." This claim cuts across the sentiment of many persons I've talked to. The eminent philosopher and mathematician, A. N. Whitehead, is also of the opposite opinion. In *Religion in the Making,* he writes:

> Religion is what the individual does with his own solitariness . . . and if you are never solitary, you are never religious. Collective enthusiasms, revivals, institutions, churches, rituals, bibles, codes of behavior, are the trappings of religion, its passing forms. They may be useful, or harmful; they may be authoritatively ordained, or merely temporary expedients. But the end of religion is beyond all this.[12]

What do you think? Does religion have to be shared by a group? If so, then there can be no such thing as a personal, private religion. Right? But then, how could a new religion ever get started? Perhaps Fromm's point is that a religion will not survive and flourish which is not shared by a group. It is certainly an accurate historical observation that religion has been almost entirely a group phenomenon, but whether it must be or ought to be is a different matter.

## MISINTERPRETATIONS OF RELIGION

The terms we have now defined are helpful for understanding religious matters, but they do not constitute a definition of religion in its authentic, healthy form. So let's keep pushing forward toward such a definition by examining some common misconceptions of religion. Against this backdrop of misconceptions the definition of authentic religion to be provided later should take on clearer, richer meaning. The two misconceptions on which we will focus are described by John Magee in his comprehensive text, *Religion and Modern Man.*

### Pseudo-Religion (Segmental Religion)

Magee reports in *Religion and Modern Man* that according to two studies of student attitudes during 1957 and 1960, religion was perceived by most students as simply one thing among many, as something they held in common with many other students, but which often came off poorly in competition with the other things bidding for their time and attention— e.g., studies, social life, sports, earning money, family. Moreover, religion was valued for the contribution it made to these other aspects of life, "but there was no hint that religion might call these other interests into question by judging them according to some higher standard. In short, religion, as they conceived it, is a useful convention for respectable people."[13]

For these students, then, religion was simply one concern among others, competing for "equal time" with education, social life, business, and family. These students have a lot of adult company, of course—adults who have a "service station" attitude toward religion: religion is what you turn to when your spirits are low and you need a fill-up; or when your oil is dirty with guilt and you want it changed; or when you want to meet like-minded persons or potential business contacts. After all, why join the smallest, poorest church in town if you sell Cadillacs for a living? In any case, religion here is thought of as a *segment* of life, lying alongside other segments rather than transcending them. It is thought of as something to be *used* for ulterior ends, rather than as something that has a bearing on the whole of life and stands in judgment on all personal and social enterprises. Clearly such a thing is not one's real religion.

Authentic religion, by contrast, should be thought of as *holistic, wholehearted,* and *transcendent.* It involves the whole person in relation to the whole of life—indeed, in relation to the whole of existence. It stands *over* the individual in judgment, and it stands *by* the individual for strength and guidance and transformation. In the light of this distinction between pseudo-religion and authentic religion, when the question arises as to what a person's religion is, it cannot be answered by simply asking him or by looking to see to what religious tradition he belongs. The question must be put on two levels: (1) what does he *think* is his religion? (2) what is *really* his religion? If what he thinks is his religion is not really his religion (according to our definition of religion), then what he *thinks* is his religion is a *pseudo-religion*. It is not his real religion.

It might seem impertinent to ask whether a person's purported religion is his real religion. After all, who should know better what Betty's religion is than Betty herself? If we don't accept her word as to what her religion is, aren't we implying that she may be deceiving us? Not necessarily. What must be kept in mind is that we are working with a functional interpretation of religion. When we ask, What is her religion? we are not asking, To what religious tradition does she belong?—we are asking, What in life does she take most seriously? What gives her integrity, purpose, and energy? What central concerns does she organize her life around and subordinate all other considerations to? She may not be aware of what her religion is in this sense. If she is not, we might provide her a valuable service by helping her distinguish it from her pseudo-religion—that is, from what she mistakenly thinks is her religion.

One has a "pseudo-religion," then, when what one thinks is one's religion is not. To be sure, it might seem strange to say of an individual that Christianity is her *pseudo-religion* whereas professional success is her *real religion*—because we do not ordinarily think of the pursuit of professional success as a religion. After the initial awkwardness, however, I think you will find the functional definition of religion more illuminating in helping you understand yourself and others than the traditional "nominal" definition, which restricts the meaning of "religion" to one of the specific religions, such as Judaism, Hinduism, etc. Once we clarify those characteristics that lead us to classify these things as religions, we must be willing to apply the word to whatever possesses those characteristics, regardless of whether or not it has been traditionally classified as a religion. (Parenthetically, as fascinating as it is to put the question, What is that person's real religion? to family and friends, you might just want to start with yourself first!)

### Crypto-Religion (Unwitting Religion)

Whereas pseudo-religion consists of thinking that your religion is one thing when it is another, crypto-religion consists in thinking that you are not religious when you are. Whereas in pseudo-religion your "professed religion" is not what gives your life integrity, zest, and direction, in crypto-religion you do not realize the religiousness of your activities because of too narrow an interpretation of religion. Consider those persons who believe that science is humanity's only means of achieving truth and happiness. Aren't those people taking a religious attitude toward science? Can't it be said meaningfully that science is their deity? This kind of attitude toward science is sometimes called "scientism" and is exemplified by persons such as Sigmund Freud and B. F. Skinner.[14] In a similar manner, the atheist who has been convinced by the Marxist interpretation of human history shows a commitment to communism which is religious in nature. Marxism provides him with a frame of orientation (dialectical materialism), an object of devotion (the Communist society), and a source of strength and transformation (the Communist party). Again, perhaps it seems odd to call communism a religion, since it rejects belief in a supreme being and is not ordinarily thought of as a religion. Yet, if we restrict usage of the word "religion" to traditions that include belief in a Supreme Person, then we cannot apply the term to Taoism or Confucianism or certain branches of Hinduism and Buddhism, because none involves belief in a supreme, personal being. If we *do* stretch the term enough to include these traditions, which *are* usually thought of as religions, then we find that it will also cover communism, scientism, and nationalism.

What do you say? Is it *ludicrous* to apply the word "religious" to systems that deny the existence of a supreme, personal being? Or is it *narrow-minded* to refuse to apply the word to systems that perform all the basic functions of theistic religions but do not include belief in a supreme, personal being?

## AUTHENTIC RELIGION

As a conclusion to these reflections on pseudo-religion and crypto-religion, let me express my conviction that *authentic religion* is not *segmental* but *holistic*—that is, related to the whole of life. Its primary virtue, as Whitehead puts it, is "a penetrating sincerity"—hence the speed and intensity with which we become disgusted by religious hypocrisy.[15] Moreover, authentic religion is not *unwitting* (something we have but are unaware of); it is *self-conscious* and *conscientious*. John Magee captures most of these points quite well when he says that a person's religion

> is what he really takes to heart as most reliably real and most convincingly valuable; it is the standard by which he judges everything else. Another way of saying this is that a man's faith is the ground upon which the rest of his life stands; it is an estimate of what is ultimately trustworthy and dependable.[16]

My own definition of religion is that it is *life lived in whole-hearted pursuit of the true and the good, and in disciplined commitment to the fruits of that pursuit.* It is a way of life that involves the whole person, that is passionate, self-conscious, disciplined, and sincere. Two of my students captured the idea quite well—one of them wrote that "to be religious . . . means a total giving of oneself to his belief" and the other wrote that religion is "a supreme interest that grows in and with you."

## TO BE FULLY HUMAN, ONE MUST BE RELIGIOUS

Before turning to other considerations, I would like to add that to refuse to be religious, in the sense we have developed, is a form of escape from becoming fully human—from facing life in *all* its ambiguity and yet living it intelligently and courageously. To be sure, most of us admit that reality is ambiguous—that is, open to various, conflicting interpretations, none of which is demonstrably true—but we refuse to admit that we must stand somewhere—that even though we cannot *prove* what is right and wrong, true and false, we must *act* as though something is true and something is good—or we perish! *Human* action is impossible apart from assumptions about the nature of reality and value. Will Herberg makes this point nicely in *Judaism and Modern Man.* "All men," he writes, "whether they know it or not, make such overall affirmations." He continues:

> For men, unlike animal creation, cannot live out their lives in the fixed patterns of nature; in their freedom, they must live to some purpose—and that purpose, however inarticulate, however primitively conceived, is in effect one's "philosophy" of life and history. A "philosophy of history" in this sense is thus no theoretical question; it is quite literally a question of existence.[17]

Without such assumptions operative in our lives, all we can do is subsist as organisms—and even that won't last very long if we do not make an assumption about the worth of being alive! Leo Tolstoy, a famous Russian novelist and religious thinker, argues this point in the following way. The answer to the question of the meaning of life can only be attained by relating the finite to the infinite, for we are finite and the reality to which we want to know our relationship is infinite. Consequently, reason is of no avail in our search for the meaning of life, for reason can relate only likes to likes—apples to apples and oranges to oranges, finite to finite and infinite to infinite. It cannot relate the finite to the infinite. Yet that is precisely what must be done if we are to get an answer to our quest for the meaning of life. There must, then, be a form of knowledge in addition to reasoning knowledge, for if there were not, we would perish for lack of a conviction regarding the meaning and worth of life. But we do not perish, so we must have a form of knowledge in addition to reasoning knowledge. "In this way," Tolstoy writes, "I was compelled to admit that, besides the reasoning knowledge, which I once thought the only true knowledge, there was in every living man another kind of knowledge, an unreasoning one—faith—which gives a possibility of living." He continues by admitting,

> All the unreasonableness of faith remained for me the same as ever, but I could not help acknowledging that faith alone gave man answers as to the questions of life, and consequently the possibility of living. Reasoning knowledge brought me to the conclusion that life was meaningless, and my life stood still, and I wished to put an end to myself.[18]

His discovery of faith put an end to that wish, instead of to his life, and he wrote that "faith is the knowledge of the meaning of human life, in consequence of which man does not destroy himself, but lives. Faith is the force of life. If a man lives, he believes in something. If he did not believe that there was something to live for, he would not live."[19] Hence, again we see that the question is not *whether* to be religious, but *how* to be religious. Which interpretation of reality should we affirm?

Your first response to this question, I believe, should not be to turn outward, in order to survey diverse interpretations of reality. Rather, it should be to turn inward, for *you already have your own fundamental beliefs about the nature of reality and value.* To be sure, it may not be clear to you what these beliefs are, but if you didn't have them, you wouldn't have made it this far in life! As Herberg puts it, "Every man . . . has his faith, whether he recognizes it or not, whether he avows it or not; the beliefs which a man really holds, it is well to remember, are not necessarily those he affirms with his mouth but those that are operative in his life."[20] Hence, you need to *make explicit* the beliefs that are *implicit* in your attitudes and actions. Why? Because it is only when these beliefs are made clear that you can *reaffirm* them, *modify* them, or *reject* them. Until they are made clear, you are to some extent a puppet, acting unwittingly according to their influence, and you are not prepared to gain maximum benefit from a study of alternative beliefs, for you will not be able to compare them clearly to your present beliefs.

Unfortunately, many of us are frightened away by philosophical bullies from a clear awareness of our own convictions. One of my students had been clearly intimidated by the prospect of articulating her beliefs, for she wrote about an article by John Wisdom, "I especially enjoyed Wisdom's article because he gave to people like me, who are so afraid to express what they think, an encouraging note that if we try to speak we might have something worthwhile to say." How oppressive to religious freedom our social environment can be! And I suspect that as our impulse to verbalize our beliefs to others withers, so does our impulse to verbalize them to ourselves. Thereby we increasingly become functions of feelings and behaviors built into us by our environments rather than of convictions freely held and consciously affirmed. The problem of self-ignorance is further compounded by our tendency to flee from facing up to our deepest convictions because of a dim awareness of the guilt that would be produced, given the gap between our convictions and our behavior, and the changes in our lives that would consequently be required.

It is possible, of course, to avoid facing up to our deepest beliefs and their likely discrepancy with our behavior, but it is no longer possible for us to hold our beliefs with the innocent certainty of a child. It is only in "bad faith" that we can say (1) that we have no beliefs about what is real and important (we have already seen why it is reasonable to assume that we do have such beliefs); or (2) that it is unimportant to clarify these beliefs to ourselves (surely you want to act on beliefs *you freely hold,* and not those that have simply been bred into you by parents, peers, teachers, and television); or (3) that it is unimportant to investigate these beliefs critically (surely you want to believe the *best* that you can discover). To be sure, you don't *have* to explicate and evaluate your beliefs. It is possible to escape from philosophic uneasiness and anguish, at least to some extent. But there is no way to do so and yet to become as fully human as you can. Escape in this instance means regression, and regression could mean that you become a permanently stunted, truncated person. Yes, passionate grappling with religious questions might make for extreme discomfort at times, but that's okay too, for as Socrates put it, "The unexamined life is not worth living," and as John Stuart Mill put it: "It is better to be a person dissatisfied than a pig satisfied; it is better to be Socrates dissatisfied than a fool satisfied." Right?

Clearly, to become religious in the above sense, to confront the question of ultimates and to launch out on an unceasing quest for and commitment to the ultimate is a demanding, strenuous thing. Perhaps it would be better to keep oneself oblivious to such problems. Perhaps you should do like the intellectual who had a philosophical aversion to exercise in any form—whenever he got the urge to exercise, he lay down until it went away! Perhaps when we get *religious* urges we should distract ourselves until they go away.

## Footnotes

1. John B. Magee, *Religion and Modern Man* (New York: Harper & Row, Publishers, 1967), p. 22.
2. One of the most fundamental divisions among people who take religion seriously is between those who believe that the only religion worthy of human commitment is one which has been *revealed by God* and those who believe

that the only religion worthy of human commitment is one which has been *created by the human community* out of the depths of its own experience and reflection. The first position is represented by Karl Barth's *Dogmatics in Outline,* and the second by John Dewey's *A Common Faith.* My intention in this book is not to favor either position, but to develop a general theory of religion in terms of which both positions can be appreciated.

3. Karl Jaspers, *Way to Wisdom* (New Haven: Yale University Press, 1954), p. 80.

4. "Lord" is used also by some translators of Oriental religious literature to refer to Buddha and Krishna, but that is probably due to the fact that the term was already being used by translators of the *Bible* to refer to the deity of Jews and of Christians. As we have seen already, Elijah, a Jew, believed that *the Lord* is God. Moreover, one of the verses of scripture most frequently uttered by Jews is the *shema,* Deuteronomy 6:4, "Hear, O Israel, the Lord our God, the Lord is One." In the New Testament, which is accepted by Christians but not Jews, "doubting" Thomas, to whom the resurrected Jesus has just appeared for the first time, is overwhelmed by the appearance of Jesus in the flesh and says to him, "My Lord and my God!" (John 20). Also, Jesus is frequently called "Lord" in the letters of the foremost Christian missionary, Paul. See, for example, his letter to the Romans, chap. 10.

5. Sarvepalli Radhakrishnan, *Recovery of Faith* (New York: Greenwood Press, 1955), p. 73.

6. Kai Nielsen, *Ethics Without God* (Buffalo: Prometheus Books, 1973), p. 17.

7. The attempt to answer these questions will lead us back into philosophy, and especially into epistemology, i.e., the theory of knowledge. Why? Because we must try to discover by what method of procedure or by what characteristics we can ascertain that a deity is God rather than an idol. This dialectic back and forth between philosophy and religion is inevitable, for it is essentially the dialectic between thought and action, evaluation and commitment.

8. Paul Tillich, *Biblical Religion and The Search for Ultimate Reality* (Chicago: The University of Chicago Press, 1955).

9. Erich Fromm, *Psychoanalysis and Religion* (New Haven: Yale University Press, 1967).

10. Ibid., p. 22.

11. Magee, *Religion and Modern Man,* p. ix.

12. Alfred North Whitehead, *Religion in the Making* (New York: World Publishing Co., 1973), pp. 16–17.

13. Magee, *Religion and Modern Man,* p. 5.

14. For an introduction to Freud's work, see his *General Introduction to Psychoanalysis* (New York: Washington Square Press, Inc., 1960). For an introduction to Skinner, see *Science and Human Behavior* (New York: The Free Press, 1953) or *Beyond Freedom and Dignity* (New York: Bantam Books, Inc., 1971).

15. Whitehead, *Religion in the Making,* p. 15.

16. Magee, *Religion and Modern Man,* p. 5.

17. Will Herberg, *Judaism and Modern Man* (New York: Atheneum, 1970), p. 198.

18. Leo Tolstoy, *My Confession,* chap. 9, any edition, or *The Religious Writings of Leo Tolstoy: Lift Up Your Eyes* (New York: The Julian Press, Inc., 1960), p. 78.

19. Tolstoy, *My Confession,* chap. 9, any edition, or *Lift Up Your Eyes,* p. 79.

20. Herberg, *Judaism and Modern Man,* p. 37.

# Roots of Religion
# in Human Existence

QUESTIONS TO THINK ABOUT

What bearings do the following aspects of human existence have on the germination of religious concern and faith?

| | |
|---|---|
| Alienation | Fear |
| Despair | Community |
| Death | Presence |
| Meaninglessness | Gratitude |
| Beliefs and Feelings | Joy |
| Emptiness | |

Religion is not something foreign to human life, something artificial, something imposed on it. It is an intimately human affair that is rooted in and grows out of human experience. What we want to do now is take a look at some of the specific aspects of human experience out of which religious concern, practice, and belief develop. Inasmuch as religion is the attempt to cope with the negative experiences and to cherish the positive experiences, the development of religious concerns, beliefs, and practices is as natural and inevitable as the development of medicine or science or art or agriculture. Moreover, even if one particular religion is a gift of divine revelation rather than of human creativity—as, for example, Islam claims— still that religion is best understood, I believe, as God's ministration to the human needs evoked by the experiences we are about to discuss.[1] Of necessity we must discuss one of these experiences first, another second, and so on, but the order in which we shall examine them in no way reflects the diversity of the order of their occurrence and importance in people's lives. For some, the catalyst of religious faith has been a negative experience— such as despair—whereas for others, it has been a positive experience— such as the feeling of community. Hence, nothing of importance should be read into the order in which we proceed.

### Alienation

The first need we shall discuss arises from the pervasive feeling of *alienation*—alienation from ourself, from others, and from existence itself. We are alienated from ourselves in the sense that we know we are not what we *ought* to be. According to our *own* best judgment, we have not done what we ought to have done. Hence, we feel *guilty,* and surely guilt is a form of self-alienation. Further, we know that we are not what we *want* to be. We would like to be more intelligent or better looking or funnier. Hence, we feel *inferior.* Indeed, sometimes we hate ourselves. Finally, sometimes we are not even sure who we are, we suffer from a lack of *identity* so that—paradoxically—we go in search of ourselves! Religion is an attempt to help us deal with these kinds of alienation, to help us cope with our guilt, self-hatred, and lack of identity, to help us become in fact what we are in essence, to help us accept ourselves for what we are, and to help us find out who we are.

As though self-alienation weren't enough to cope with, we are alienated also from others. To be sure, we *say* that "what the world needs now is love, sweet love," but when it comes down to the nitty-gritty of our daily lives, we find ourselves caught in crushing competition with one another and we find ourselves alienated from one another by envy and contempt. Further, when it comes to laying our money and time on the line for those who are desperately in need, we all too often find ourselves profoundly indifferent. Religion is an attempt to get at the roots of our alienation from on another and to bring about reconciliation, caring, and commitment.

Finally, we feel alienated from the power or powers that are responsible for our existence. Without having asked for it, we have been thrown into existence, surrounded with circumstances with which we must struggle, desperately at times, and over which we have little control. We are burdened with physical features that are frequently not to our liking, tormented with various forms of suffering, and plagued by passions that destroy our peace of mind and threaten what social adjustment we do manage to achieve. All of this and then we are crushed by death. Alienated? You better believe it! But must it remain that way? Is *indifference* or *hostility* our only possible attitude toward the power or powers that are responsible for our existence? The great religions insist that there is another way, a positive way. Alfred North Whitehead, speaking from a western theistic tradition, put it like this: when we begin our religious journey God is a *void* to us—a matter of indifference. As we progress we perceive God as *enemy*— for He judges our desires and our actions, and He leaves our deepest questions unanswered. But if we move forward intrepidly, we come to know God as *companion.* Indifference and hostility are transcended, even though questions and yearnings remain.[2]

### Despair

Religious concern is also awakened by the experience of *despair.* Sometimes we despair of *finding* the good. We don't know what to do; we have not on our own been able to discover what to do; and we do not want to act arbitrarily. We want to do that which is good and right, but we have no conviction as to what it is. If we do not despair completely, we wait in hope that the nature of the good and the right will be revealed to us, will impress itself upon us. Yet should *this* occur, we become liable to another kind of despair—namely, the kind that results when we find ourselves *unable* to do that which in our own opinion is right. It might be that we do not feel *strong* enough to do what is required or, more seriously, it might be that we find ourselves perversely *betraying* our own sense of the right. Experiences such as these take on religious significance by causing us to look beyond ourselves for some source of strength or transformation in order that we can do what we believe we ought to do and be what we most deeply want to be.

### Death

Another source of despair is *death.* You and I know that we will die and that there is nothing we can do to avoid ultimate death—no matter how undesirable or outrageous it might seem. Our reaction against impending death leads us to ask questions about ourselves and about the power or powers that have brought us into being. Clearly, my body will die—but am I identical with my body? Perhaps I can survive the disintegration of my body? At least one four-year-old, my youngest son, Christopher, seems to think so. I was undressing him for bed one evening and said to him as I removed his footwear, "Off with your shoe! Off with your sock!" Then, without malice or forethought, I tugged at his foot and said "Off with your foot!" Well, he thought that was great fun, so we had to do it with his other foot, his legs, hands, and arms! Then he made a request that I, constrained by more rigid modes of thought, would never have thought of. He said with a twinkle in his eye, "Now take off my body!" So I put my hands around his waist and pretended to lift off the remainder of his body and place it to one side. Then I asked, "Now where are you?" and he broke into great laughter, which I couldn't help joining. Having nothing left to remove, I dressed what remained and it was "lights off." Despite the intuitions of four-year-olds there are, oddly enough, adults who doubt that the self can be separated from the body. Still, even if they are correct, perhaps the power or powers that have brought me into being in the first place can bring me into being again.[3] And even if that is not possible— that is, if the sun of consciousness shall never dawn for me again after my death—is there, perhaps, a power which will sustain the good I have accomplished and which will favor the efforts of all those who struggle on behalf of justice, peace, and brotherhood? Clearly, one could use such questions as springboards into escapist fantasy, but just as surely one can accept the ambiguities of our situation and still hope that death is not the end, that cruelty doesn't ultimately have as firm a place in reality as kindness, and that indifference is not the final word which shall be pronounced over all things.

If we do become convinced that the worst is true, then a pall is cast over our lives. As a college student who committed suicide stated in a farewell note, "I'm going to die anyway." Why not now rather than later? Why run the gauntlet of life since no matter how successful we are at avoiding pain and achieving pleasure, upon our death it will not matter how much pleasure we enjoyed, since there will be no remembrance of good times past? The problem becomes especially urgent when one becomes aware of the scientific prediction that eventually *all* life will be destroyed in a cosmic collapse. Hence, even our contributions to posterity will come to naught. Surely this prospect must have some kind of reflexive influence upon the way we feel about ourselves, other persons, and our contributions to them. A wry comment by retired heavyweight boxing champion Jack Sharkey, at age seventy, seems relevant to this point. Sharkey, living in retirement in a small New Hampshire town, replied to an interviewer, "I've got everything I need here. The doctor lives across the street, the druggist is on the corner, the funeral parlor is nearby, and the cemetery is right up the street." In the light of such a comment we can understand better why John Magee writes, "The sting of death, then, is the poisoning of hope, the extinguishing of all possibility of a full human existence here and now."[4] Do you agree?

### Meaninglessness

A further source of religious awakening, a source closely related to the fact of death, is the sense of *meaninglessness* that haunts us from time to time. As Magee puts it,

> Life without ultimate significance is not only flat and stale, it leads finally to the negation of life itself. People lose heart even in the midst of success and

physical well-being when they are convinced that their existence is meaningless. A person with a fine car but no place to go can hardly be happy. Similarly, a human being with all the means of life [money, looks, talent, ambition, but who sees no point to his life as a whole] will find himself in ever deepening frustration.[5]

The great religions are attempts to meet this need for meaning, to provide a framework within which our lives are graced with significance, to provide a foundation to which we can anchor ourselves in an infinite and sometimes stormy ocean. Walt Whitman, nineteenth-century American poet, brings out by analogy the nature of our ceaseless and sometimes desperate search for meaning:

A noiseless patient spider,
I mark'd where on a little promontory it stood isolated,
Mark'd how to explore the vacant vast surrounding,
It launch'd forth filament, filament, filament out of itself,
Ever unreeling them, ever tirelessly speeding them.
And you O my soul where you stand,
Surrounded, detached, in measureless oceans of space,
Ceaselessly musing, venturing, throwing, seeking the spheres to connect them,
Till the bridge you will need be form'd, till the ductile anchor hold,
Till the gossamer thread you fling catch somewhere, O my soul.[6]

### Beliefs and Feelings

You might want to take a moment here to think about whether one's *understanding* of reality has any necessary reflexive influence on one's *feelings* about oneself, others, and the future. That is, do beliefs have any necessary, predictable influence on feelings? Most people, including myself, would answer "yes," I believe. Yet there seems to be some disagreement. For example, can a naturalistic faith (no personal God; Nature is everything) be as optimistic and rewarding as a theistic faith? Kai Nielsen, a Canadian philosopher, argues that it can be. He states in *Ethics Without God* that an atheist "with secular knowledge alone can find clear and permanent sources of happiness such that whoever will avail himself of these sources of happiness can, if he is fortunate, lead a happy and purposeful life."[7] Bertrand Russell, British philosopher, mathematician, and social critic, disagrees, though he also believes that modern science has discredited theism. Hence, he wrote in his 1903 essay, "A Free Man's Worship":

That man is the product of causes which had no prevision of the end they were achieving; that his origin, his growth, his hopes and fears, his loves and his beliefs, are but the outcome of accidental collocations of atoms; that no fire, no heroism, no intensity of thought and feeling, can preserve an individual life beyond the grave; that all the labors of the ages, all the devotion, all the inspiration, all the noonday brightness of human genius, are destined to extinction in the vast death of the solar system, and that the whole temple of man's achievement must inevitably be buried beneath the debris of a universe in ruins—all these things, if not quite beyond dispute, are yet [due to scientific investigation, Russell was convinced] so nearly certain, that no philosophy which rejects them can hope to stand. Only within the scaffolding of these truths, only on the firm foundation of unyielding despair, can the soul's habitation henceforth be safely built.[8]

Ernst Nagel, distinguished philosopher of science, has made a more recent statement to the same effect, and therefore to some extent in disagreement with Nielsen's optimism. Nagel wrote:

> Though slavish resignation to remediable ills is not characteristic of atheistic thought, responsible atheists have never pretended that human effort can invariably achieve the heart's every legitimate desire. A tragic view of life is thus an uneliminable ingredient in atheistic thought. This ingredient does not invite or generally produce lugubrious lamentation. But it does touch the atheist's view of man and his place in nature with an emotion that makes the philosophical atheist a kindred spirit to those who . . . have developed a serenely resigned attitude toward the inevitable tragedies of the human estate.[9]

I encourage you to consider this question of the relation between beliefs and feelings because the way a religion makes you feel about yourself, others, and the future is a very real and a very important aspect of it, and different religions make us feel differently. To be sure, we shouldn't choose a religion simply because it makes us feel good. Religions include beliefs, and the question of the truth or falsity of beliefs cannot be settled by how good or bad they make us feel. Yet because the truth or falsity of a religion is a very difficult thing to establish with finality, I believe you will find that in choosing a religion your feelings play a legitimately more important role than they do in other contexts, such as the scientific laboratory, where they may be totally irrelevant.

### Emptiness

Moving right along, whereas in the problem of meaninglessness the prominent need is for a satisfying *intellectual* understanding of reality, in the problem of "emptiness" the need is primarily *emotional.* It is the need to *feel* uplifted and filled. Such emptiness is marked by a kind of spiritual hunger, by a restless search for food that satisfies. St. Augustine (354–430 A.D.) captured this experience in words when he said in a prayer in his *Confessions,* "Thou hast made us for Thyself, and our hearts are restless till they find their rest in Thee." In the same spirit, members of a contemporary Pentecostal group have told me that God creates us with an infinite void within and that nothing but God can fill that void—no matter how desperately we try to fill it with other things. Whether these people are correct that only the Christian God can fill the void is a question we shall not pursue in this book. But the experience of emptiness they talk about and the fact that religion endeavors to fill that emptiness seem to be universal facts. As John Magee puts it, man needs "a deep sense of well-being, an experience of joy, happiness, even ecstasy, that will not crumble under the attrition of life."[10] I would like to summarize this by saying that we sometimes feel the need of a sense of *buoyancy*. It is a sense of being unsinkable, even in a storm. Only when we have this feeling within us shall we have the *guts* to live courageously in the face of adversity; only then shall we have the *single-mindedness* to ignore the petty annoyances of life and to resist its trivial distractions; only then shall we have the *resilience* to pick ourselves up and start afresh after failure or tragedy. Religion is devoted to the acquisition of this pervasive sense of buoyancy.

### *Fear*

Parenthetically, there are those who say that *fear* is the primary source of religion. Bertrand Russell, for example, says, "Fear is the basis of the whole thing—fear of the mysterious, fear of defeat, fear of death."[11] That seems simplistic to me. The emergence of religion, I am suggesting, is the result of many different factors, both negative and positive. Though we have focused on the negative thus far, shortly we shall take a look at positive sources of religion. Nonetheless, I agree that fear has been a real and understandable source of religious thought and practice. People fear that they will not be able to withstand the suffering imposed on them by life, so they turn to an extraordinary source of strength and endurance. They fear that the values they are struggling to advance in this life may be destroyed by evil forces or indifferent matter, so they hope that there are forces of good which will prevail and can be tapped even now. People fear that they may be held responsible after death for the way they live before death, so they try to discover the will of the gods and to act accordingly. All of these are reasonable responses to our human situation. We need not apologize for them. Further, it seems to me that of the three types of fear which Russell specifies as sources of religion, only one, "fear of defeat," is accurate. Regarding fear of the mysterious, people do not fear the mysterious simply because it is mysterious. Entry into the mysterious can be exhilarating as well as frightening. It all depends on one's intuitions and preconceptions. The mysterious can be alluring as well as alarming. One fears the mysterious only when one has an intuition that "bad things are going to happen" as a result of it or when one already has a world view which holds that the denizens of the mysterious are our enemies. No doubt fear of the mysterious has given rise to some religious beliefs and practices, but so, according to my observation, has love of the mysterious. Perhaps the most lovely expression of this fact is a statement by Albert Einstein, scientific genius and sensitive religious spirit. He wrote:

> The most beautiful thing that we can experience is the mysterious. It is the source of all true art and science. He to whom this emotion is a stranger, who

can no longer pause to wonder and stand, wrapped in awe, is as good as dead; his mind and his eyes are closed. The insight into the mystery of life, coupled though it be with fear, has also given rise to religion. To know that what is impenetrable to us really exists, manifesting itself as the highest wisdom and the most radiant beauty which our dull faculties can comprehend only in their most primitive form—this knowledge, this feeling, is at the center of true religiousness.[12]

Regarding fear of death, I do not believe it is accurate to say that people fear death at all! Why? Because fear is fear of an experience—e.g., being bitten by a snake. Now let's divide everyone into two groups and see if either group can rightfully be said to fear death. The two groups are (1) those who believe there is no life after death, and (2) those who do believe there is life after death. Those who believe there is no life after death will not fear death, I submit, for death is not an experience which we have. It is true that one of my students once wrote, "Nobody is certain or will ever be certain of exactly what follows death. We can only know for sure when we die." But that seems all wrong to me. Dying is not an experience; it is the end of experience. Hence, it is nothing to be feared. It is, to most of us, something to be *abhorred,* which means literally, "to shrink from," but that is precisely because it is not itself an experience but the end of experience. After all, if you're having a good time and believe that death is the end of good times, bad times, and any times at all, then you'll "shrink from" death; indeed, you'll run from it and fight against it. But it's not correct to say you'll fear it, for, we are assuming, you believe that death causes neither pain nor pleasure, but the total absence of consciousness.

Okay, so those who do not believe in life after death will not fear death, though they may abhor it. But what about those who do believe that there is life after death? Again it seems inaccurate to say that this second group fears death. Some people who believe in life after death welcome death, for they believe it is the portal to paradise! Other people are made anxious by "the gnawing tooth of time" because they fear not death but what they believe lies beyond it—e.g., judgment and punishment by the gods or God. Hence, here too it seems to me that Russell's explanation of the origin of religion is simplistic. Love of life and love of death have had as much to do with the origin of religion as have fear of life and fear of death, and perhaps more so.

### Community

Another source of religion to which John Magee points is man's need for *communion.* Sociologists have long been aware of the profound extent to which people participate in religious groups for the sake of the sense of community it provides them. Religions provide people with an opportunity to come together in a noncompetitive, nonutilitarian context which affirms their worth and their oneness, which encourages them to become involved in spite of timidity. Indeed, Martin Buber, Jewish existentialist, teaches that the best way to serve God is to build community.[13] Religious community is usually more than social, though. Loneliness can be cosmic as well as social. If we cannot say "Thou" to the universe which surrounds us, we experience that profound emptiness we spoke of earlier. Why? Because we are made for communion—for that kinship with all being which we sense in the beauty of the universe, for companionship with everything that lives, for "communion with the total soul of things."[14] Clearly, it is religion which endeavors to lead us to this sense of cosmic oneness.

### Presence

Whereas religious *concern* grows out of such needs as the above, religious *faith* grows out of the moments in which these needs are ministered to—moments when guilt is replaced by forgiveness, confusion by direction, self-hatred by self-acceptance, despair by hope. Since we have just spoken of our desire for a sense of oneness with the powers that be, consider the positive experience of a divine presence reported by persons throughout human history and across the face of the globe. Such experiences have not always been preceded by an intense feeling of need, but they have always created the conviction that one was in the presence of a divine person. Simone Weil, a very unusual woman, wrote of her first religious experience, "God had mercifully prevented me from reading the mystics, so that it would be clear to me that I had not fabricated an absolutely unexpected encounter."[15] Of that first experience, she wrote:

> In a moment of intense physical suffering, when I was forcing myself to feel love, but without desiring to give a name to that love, I felt, without being in any way prepared for it (for I had never read the mystical writers) a presence more personal, more certain, more real than that of a human being, though inaccessible to the senses and the imagination.[16]

In Chapter 8 we shall return to the topic of religious experience and look at naturalistic as well as theistic interpretations of it. Meanwhile, it should be clear how religious faith and practice emerge from such experiences as those of Simone Weil.

### Gratitude

Another contributor to the germination of religion is the experience of *gratitude*, which we have occasionally toward reality itself, rather than toward a specific person. Because we feel grateful for our existence and for life itself, we give our thanks "to whom it may concern." G. K. Chesterton, British novelist and biographer of such persons as St. Francis and St.

Thomas Aquinas, reported on one of his own experiences in the following passage from *Orthodoxy:*

> The test of all happiness is gratitude; and I felt grateful, though I hardly knew to whom. Children are grateful when Santa Claus puts in their stocking gifts of toys or sweets. Could I not be grateful to Santa Claus when he put in my stockings the gift of two miraculous legs? We thank people for birthday presents of cigars and slippers. Can I thank no one for the birthday present of birth?[17]

Again it is understandable that such feelings of gratitude should become part of a religious faith and give rise to such rites as offering and prayer.

### Joy

Finally, how could we close a discussion of sources of religious belief and practice without mentioning the experience of joy? I do not mean the joy that comes from identifiable sources, such as having one's marriage proposal accepted or playing a beautiful piece of music. Rather, I am referring to the joy that flows over us, that fills us, we know not whence or why. It is perhaps this experience above all others that is the pulsating heart of religious life. Moses, Jesus, Mohammed, and the Hindu mystics all speak of the joy that passes understanding—the joy that is available to us through certain beliefs and/or practices. Indeed, how can a religion *not* grow out of such experiences?

These, then, are some of the needs and experiences out of which religious concern and faith emerge. The list is not complete, and I hope you'll take a moment to see what others you can think of. Certainly on a fuller list would be included the *comfort* religion has traditionally provided to those in grief, distress, or depression; the *values* religion provides us with which to guide our lives and nurture our children; the *significance* accorded to work and creativity; and the ability to *hope* in hopeless situations. Perhaps the most intriguing source of religious faith mentioned to me, by my friend Mildred Carver, was *family loyalty.* At first I was simply puzzled, but the idea is growing on me with increasing persuasiveness. Certainly the language of the family has played a central role in the endeavors of nearly all religions to explain our proper relations to one another and to the absolute. Further, someone who has had a good family experience is probably in a much better position to appreciate the concepts of human solidarity, forgiveness, trust, and so on. In brief, as long as human existence continues to be characterized by such needs and experiences as we have discussed, people will continue to awaken religiously and to cherish and transmit those religious practices, beliefs, and symbols which enable them to live more richly.[18]

**Footnotes**

1. Much of our discussion shall draw on Part Seven of John B. Magee, *Religion and Modern Man* (New York: Harper & Row, Publishers, 1967).

2. Alfred North Whitehead, *Religion in the Making* (New York: World Publishing Co., 1973), p. 16. My friend Harriet Cramton, who is fascinated by children and religion, taken together as well as individually, has sometimes objected that my points are true enough of adults but not of children. For example, she pointed out (and I agree) that a child who is reared in a home of love and faith will know God initially as companion, not enemy. Still, she allows, it is quite common in our society for people to be expelled from the spiritual world of their childhood into the doubts and negations of adolescence, wherein God is often perceived as void or enemy.

3. The first possibility, survival by the soul of death of the body, is commonly called "immortality," whereas the second possibility, re-creation of the bodily self subsequent to real annihilation at death, is called "resurrection." For an introduction to the differences between these two conceptions of life after death see Krister Stendahl, ed., *Immortality and Resurrection* (New York: The Macmillan Company, 1965).

4. Magee, *Religion and Modern Man,* p. 476.

5. Ibid., p. 35.

6. Gay Wilson Allen and Charles T. Davis, eds., *Walt Whitman's Poems* (New York: Grove Press, Inc., 1959), p. 198.

7. Kai Nielsen, *Ethics Without God* (Buffalo: Prometheus Books, 1973), p. 58.

8. Bertrand Russell, *Why I Am Not a Christian* (New York: Simon and Schuster, Inc., 1957), p. 107.

9. J. E. Fairchild, ed., *Basic Beliefs: The Religious Philosophies of Mankind* (New York: Sheridan House, Inc., 1959), p. 186.

10. Magee, *Religion and Modern Man,* p. 36.

11. Russell, *Why I Am Not a Christian,* p. 22.

12. Louis Untermeyer, *Makers of the Modern World* (New York: Simon and Schuster, Inc., 1955), pp. 540–541.

13. Martin Buber, *Paths in Utopia* (Boston: Beacon Press, 1958), p. xvi.

14. William James, *The Will to Believe and Other Essays in Popular Philosophy* (New York: Dover Publications, Inc., 1956), p. 40. See also Magee, *Religion and Modern Man,* pp. 449–450, 485–492.

15. Simone Weil, *Waiting for God* (New York: Capricorn Books, 1951), p. 25.

16. Ibid., p. 24.

17. Gilbert K. Chesterton, *Orthodoxy* (Garden City, N.Y.: Image Books, 1959), p. 55.

18. An interesting analysis of the impact of the family experience on the development of religious faith can be found in "The Development of Ritualization" by psychiatrist Erik H. Erikson, in *The Religious Situation: 1968,* Donald R. Cutler, ed. (Boston: Beacon Press, 1968), pp. 711–33.

# Traits of a Healthy Religious Faith

- What is *emotional integrity* and why is it a trait of a healthy religion?
- What are some of the personal and social consequences of unresolved inner conflicts?
- What is *intellectual integrity* and why is it a necessary trait of a healthy religion?
- What is the relation of *doubt* to a healthy religious faith?
- If science is true, is religion false?
- Are humanism and religion incompatible?
- Is religion "the opiate of the masses"?
- How does a healthy religion deal with the problem of evil?
- In what sense is a healthy religion optimistic? What would be the opposite?
- Wherein lies the value of beliefs that "bake no bread"?
- Is there both a bad sense and a good sense in which religion can be a crutch?
- In what sense is a healthy religion a mode of creativity?

Clearly, if the tack we have been taking is correct, then it is no longer meaningful to ask, Should I be religious? Now it is appropriate only to ask, *How* should I be religious? I, as an individual, have no authority to answer that question for you, as an individual. Still, I do believe that certain traits are characteristic of any religious faith that is healthy. Hence, I would like to see your faith, whatever final form it takes, fall within the boundaries established by these traits. Consequently, I would like to set forth some of these traits and elicit your reaction. You may wish to add additional traits or to remove some of mine. I ask only that you self-consciously *justify* your additions and removals to the best of your ability.


## EMOTIONAL INTEGRITY

The first characteristic we shall look at is *emotional integrity.* A healthy religion is one that draws all our energies unto one object, one goal, one God. The life of the individual is *unified* by a single object of devotion, but it is *fragmented* by multiple incompatible objects. If your own life is divided within, if your mind and heart are the arena of severe conflicts, it is probably because you are attracted to incompatible objects of commitment. The conflict will not be resolved until one of the objects becomes appreciated as superior to the others or until yet another object appears and causes your interest in the competing objects to disappear, even as the sun causes the stars to vanish at dawn. An inner conflict, then, should always lead us to the following considerations: (1) are all of the alternatives really equally worthy of my commitment, even after the most rigorous analysis? (2) is there some new alternative that might banish the conflict by making me lose my interest in the present alternatives?

It is important to transcend such conflicts and achieve emotional unity because inner conflicts are among the chief causes of personal misery and social disruption. Why? Because people afflicted with an inner conflict of loyalties tend to be burdened with (1) *confusion,* because they do not know to which object to commit themselves, and (2) *guilt,* because no matter to which object they commit themselves, they still feel sufficiently attracted to the other objects to suffer guilt at having betrayed them; further, either (3) such persons tend to transform their guilt and confusion into *hostility,* which is projected upon themselves or the world (making other people miserable), or (4) they tend to escape into *apathy,* so as not to feel the torment of indecision, of confusion, and of guilt. Perhaps the extreme form of apathy is found in the person who withdraws from interaction with the world to the literal extreme of lying unresponsively in a fetal position.

Hence, the wisdom of the commandment in Exodus 20:3, "You shall have no other gods before me." Why? Because having more than one god will tear you apart! As we are *unified* by one object of commitment, we are *torn asunder* by two or more. Søren Kierkegaard captured this idea in the title of one of his books: *Purity of Heart is to Will One Thing.* This doesn't mean, of course, that we cannot be committed to parents, mate, children, benevolent causes, justice, and so on, because they are multiple objects of commitment. The single, transcendent commitment of which I speak is one that enables us to unite all these other commitments in a harmonious way. I submit, then, that there is no other way to become whole, to be fully released, to be drawn out into life to the full extent of our capacities except by a single object of devotion which releases, directs, and harmonizes all of our energies for its own sake. I cannot tell you what that object is for you. You must discover it yourself. But it does seem to me that to be religious is to believe that there *is* something real enough and sacred enough to release our energies and unify our lives. Whoever despairs of this possibility despairs of religious faith and must perceive religious longing as a cruel and answerless question.

## INTELLECTUAL INTEGRITY

A second trait of a healthy religious faith is that it does not contradict one's sense of *intellectual integrity*. The emotional integrity that is required and created by devotion to one and only one God must be matched by intellectual integrity. A person cannot achieve wholeness if he believes that his religion or his deity requires him to believe that which is contrary to logic or fact. More specifically, it seems to me that we sacrifice our intellectual integrity whenever we affirm that as true which we know is false, believe is false, suspect is false, or know we aren't sure about, and when we attribute to a proposition a greater degree of probability than we believe the evidence really warrants. Intellectual integrity is a precious part of personal wholeness and should not be sacrificed on the altar of church or temple membership. If it is, it will return to haunt us in the form of hostility toward ourselves for having made such a sacrifice and hostility toward our religious tradition for having required such a sacrifice. Nothing is worth the price of your sense of self-respect. This does not mean, however, that you must choose between religious faith and intellectual integrity. To be sure, some people believe otherwise. Bertrand Russell quips that faith is "believin' what you know ain't so," and Friedrich Nietzsche says that to have faith is "to will to not know the truth." I disagree, and so does Paul Tillich, who writes in *Biblical Religion and the Search for Ultimate Reality:*

> Faith and doubt do not essentially contradict each other. Faith is the continuous tension between itself and the doubt within itself. This tension does

not always reach the strength of a struggle; but, latently, it is always present. . . . Faith includes both an immediate awareness of something unconditional and the courage to take the risk of uncertainty upon itself. Faith says "Yes," in spite of the anxiety of "No." It does not remove the "No" of doubt and the anxiety of doubt; it does not build a castle of doubt-free security—only a neurotically distorted faith does that—but it takes the "No" of doubt and the anxiety of insecurity into itself.[1]

Hence, a mature faith does not fear radical doubt. It confronts it. Indeed, it grows out of it or over against it. Doubt is a *structural feature* of a healthy, mature religious faith, for we do not want to commit ourselves absolutely to that which is less than the absolute.[2] Hence, we must doubt: we must scrutinize that to which we are *asked* to commit ourselves, and we must scrutinize that to which we *have* already committed ourselves. Why? In order that we may be continually assured that that to which we are committed *is in our judgment* at the moment the best to which we *can* be committed. Hence, we should affirm the best that we know while keeping ourselves open to the possibility of something better. If we don't affirm the best that we know, we can only affirm something less or affirm nothing at all. Surely we don't want to affirm anything less than the best we know, and we earlier saw the consequences of affirming nothing at all. Further, if we don't keep ourselves open to the possibility of something better, we exclude ourselves from it if it does exist, and we likely become dogmatic about the finality of that to which we are committed.

Before we leave the trait of intellectual integrity, let's think for a moment about the so-called conflict between religion and science. Is it the case that if science is true, then religion is false? I think not. In the first case, the statement is too broad, since by "religion" most people would mean the concrete religions of the world, and these are too diverse to be joined together by any creed (1) which they all affirm in common and (2) which stands opposed to science. Further, if my own definition of religion is accepted, then science and religion should not contradict one another. Rather, they should supplement one another, for they perform basically different human functions. Science is intent on discovering the causal relations between those kinds of things which can be sensed directly or detected by instruments, things such as gases and metals (molecules and light waves), whereas religion is intent on discovering those forces and ideas which enable us to live as fully as possible. In one sense, science can be subsumed within the enterprise of religion, for science is a means to living more fully. Insofar as one engages in scientific activity in order that people can live more fully, one's scientific activity could be considered religious. Both enterprises are also engaged, however, in constructing a frame of orientation, and it is here that they have clashed over such issues as the creation of the universe, evolution, and the nature of mankind. It now seems clear that whenever science and religion do overlap and a religion makes a claim which can be investigated by scientific means, that claim should not be withheld from (and perhaps *should* be submitted to) such investigation. Further, if the claim, such as geocentrism, is discredited by science, then it should be rejected. When the results of a scientific investigation of a religious belief are *not* conclusive, however, it should not be assumed that one has a moral or intellectual obligation to abjure the belief until it *is* proved true by science. When a matter of belief is urgent to you, you have the right to believe as seems best to you until the truth is made clear, if it can be made clear by reason and evidence. That salt melts ice is clearly demonstrable. That persons determine some of their actions by their freedom of will is not so clearly demonstrable. Even more significantly, are there types of claims that are completely outside the boundaries of scientific investigation? Are scientific methods even applicable, for example, to the proof or disproof of the existence of the biblical Lord? Further, can we by means of scientific methods prove that our senses reveal the way the world "really" is—or even that there really is a world apart from our perceptions? We won't belabor these points, for this is not an essay in metaphysics or philosophy of science. I would only urge you to be aware that not all that is claimed in the name of science is a matter of science. Perhaps the best antidote to naive optimism about the omniscience of science is a good dose of philosophy of science.

Parenthetically, an interesting question was raised in a paper by one of my students. "How," she asked, "can some invisible supernatural being create the entire universe with all its peculiarities in six days, no less?" One of the issues she is raising is this: How can something that is nonsensory *be* anything and *do* anything? A good question, yet I doubt that she discounts the reality of her own consciousness and the effectiveness of her own will, though the reality of neither is capable of being demonstrated by means of sensation. Further, the religious person should not be disoriented by the discovery of regularities in nature and of our ability, within limits, to control natural processes. We should be glad that the world is largely dependable and that we can improve and control it for our survival and pleasure. It would be naive, though, to conclude that because nature is dependable and we can control it to some extent, the solution to *all* our problems is just a matter of science and time. Scientific methods and discoveries can be used for weal or woe, and we, as a species, have a notorious record for working woe. Hence, we stand in need of something which will influence us so that we will use scientific methods and knowledge in intelligent and humane ways. Perhaps devotion to science itself is the means by which we can be transformed into a species of intelligent, compassionate individuals. B. F. Skinner appears to hold this point of view. Yet surely it is not obvious that devotion to science affects us in this way. If it can, then it should be our deity, our object of religious devotion. But is it science, the Lord, humanity, communism, or something else to which we must submit ourselves in order to achieve a good life, individually and socially? That is the religious question. People have answered differently and will continue to do so until one answer is demonstrated to be objectively superior to all others.

One final word about intellectual integrity. I do not believe it is incompatible with a sense of mystery and even of paradox. Regarding mystery, recall the statement by Einstein. Also, consider the following argument by Baron Friedrich von Hügel, nineteenth-century lay theologian, to the effect that a sense of mystery in religion is understandably inevitable. After a reference to the level of awareness a dog would have of its master's activities—e.g., repairing a clock or composing a poem—von Hügel wrote:

> The source and object of religion, if religion be true and its object be real, *cannot,* indeed, *by any possibility, be as clear to me even as I am to my dog.* For the cases we have considered deal with realities inferior to our own reality (material objects, or animals), or with realities level to our own reality (fellow human beings), or with realities no higher above ourselves than are we, finite human beings, to our very finite dogs. Whereas, in the case of religion—if religion be right—we apprehend and affirm realities indefinitely superior in quality and amount of reality to ourselves, and which, nevertheless (or rather, just because of this), anticipate, penetrate, and sustain us with a quite unpicturable intimacy. The obscurity of my life to my dog must thus be greatly exceeded by the obscurity of the life of God to me. Indeed the obscurity of plant life—so obscure for my mind, because so indefinitely inferior and poorer than is my human life—must be greatly exceeded by the dimness, for my human life, of God—of His reality and life, so different and superior, so unspeakably more rich and alive, than is, or ever can be, my own life and reality.[3]

Regarding paradox, consider the fact that contemporary physicists treat light as both a wave and a particle, because it has properties of both; yet there is no known way to make sense of the statement that light is both a wave and a particle! Perhaps the paradox will be resolved, and perhaps it won't, but in a conflict between fact and logic, it is fact that should be given the upper hand.[4] The broader significance of this point is that we should not allow the intellect to impoverish our lives when its categories are too narrow to cover the facts of our experience or the richness of a multifaceted reality that stretches beyond the categories of the mind. Logic is part of life, but life is more than logic. The whole is greater than the part. As John Henry Cardinal Newman put it, there is a kind of logic that does us a great disservice by dispelling our legitimate sense of mystery and paradox. How does it do this? By trivializing the profound and dismissing the difficult. "One is not at all pleased," he wrote, "when poetry, or eloquence, or devotion, is considered as if chiefly intended to feed syllogisms."[5] Newman, a nineteenth-century cardinal in the Church of Rome, also insisted that the intellectual difficulties of a doctrine do not mean necessarily that we should doubt the truth of the doctrine. Having in mind the difficult doctrines of his Christian faith—e.g., the Trinity and transubstantiation, he wrote:

> Ten thousand difficulties do not make one doubt, as I understand the subject; difficulty and doubt are incommensurate. There of course may be difficulties in the evidence; but I am speaking of difficulties intrinsic to the doctrines, or to their compatibility with each other. A man may be annoyed that he cannot work out a mathematical problem, of which the answer is or is not given to him, without doubting that it admits of an answer, or that a particular answer is the true one.[6]

Hence, the intellectual difficulties generated by the mysteries and paradoxes of a religious doctrine do not entail that we must reject the doctrine in order to preserve our intellectual integrity. Indeed, intellectual integrity may *require* that we affirm a mystery or paradox, rather than deny an aspect of our sense of reality.[7]

## HUMANISTIC

A third trait of healthy religion is that it is *humanistic.* If you are used to thinking of humanism as an atheistic, anti-religious movement, then you might think once again that I am trying to mix oil and water. But if we take the core of humanism to be *concern for and commitment to the universal welfare of human beings,* then I would say that humanism and a healthy religion are not only compatible but inseparable! Martin Buber put this point beautifully in the title of one of his books: *Believing Humanism.* I propose to you, then, that a healthy religion—theistic, atheistic, or otherwise—will be humanistic. It will emphasize *maximization of the quality of life on earth for all persons.* Alfred North Whitehead, in *Religion in the Making,* contends that enjoyment is the *purpose* of life, that God has brought us into being precisely in order that we might enjoy being![8] Milton Steinberg goes a step further in *Basic Judaism* and says that we have a God-given *duty* to enjoy life and that it is part of religion's function to help us do so![9] Does this purpose, this duty imply a life of crude sensualism? Not at all, for there are the joys of fellowship, of work, of creativity, and of worship, as well as of the body. Further, an intelligent religion does not limit itself to self-gratification, but involves itself also in the creation, maintenance, and improvement of a system of natural and social relations which makes *universal* enjoyment possible. That is, the healthy and intelligent religious person is not fixated on immediate selfish pleasure, without regard for others. Such a person finds pleasure also in bringing pleasure to others, whether directly, as in the case of the chef or entertainer, or indirectly, as in the case of the community planner or ecologist who helps create and maintain an entire environment of diverse opportunities for the enjoyment of nature and society. This means, of course, that an intelligent religion opposes those things which demean or exploit people and which prevent them from enjoying existence in a manner compatible with universal enjoyment.

Karl Marx, the founder of modern communism, had a very different understanding of religion.[10] He described it as "the opiate of the masses," and he made a very important point—namely, that the idea of "heaven" can be used to exploit people, to desensitize them, to manipulate them. It is a simple historical fact, for example, that wealthy slave owners favored and supported ministers who taught the slaves that *industriousness* at work and *obedience* to one's superiors will be rewarded "with pie in the sky, bye and bye." Then too, consider the teachings that the riches of this life are not to be compared to the riches of the next life (so don't worry about your poverty during this brief life), and that it will be as hard for the rich to get into heaven as for a camel to pass through the eye of a needle (so be glad you aren't rich, because being rich in this life makes it more difficult to get into heaven, and because the riches of this life last only a few decades, whereas the riches of the next life last forever!). You can see how such teachings, all adapted from the New Testament, could be used to manipulate the poor by making them reluctant to rebel or loaf, by taking their attention off their plight in this life, focusing their attention on the rewards of the next life, and by making their poverty seem an asset. I agree with Marx that such preachments are an "opiate of the masses," used to maintain them in a slavish stupor, but I also believe that such preachments represent a *perversion* of religion. Religion doesn't *have* to be an opiate. It can be a stimulant. Indeed, healthy forms of religion are the *mainstay* of the hope of the masses, for these forms of religion insist on the *dignity* of every person, on the *brother/sisterhood* of all persons, on their *responsibility* for one another, and on their *right* to enjoy their existence. Finally, I do not see how Marx's theory of religion can satisfactorily explain such religious political activists as Mahatma Gandhi and Martin Luther King, Jr. Religion didn't put them to sleep. It roused them to action.[11]

REALISTIC ABOUT EVIL

A fourth trait of a healthy religion is that it is *realistic* about evil and *helpful* in the face of it. As I will argue shortly, it is a mistake to "get hung up" on evil, to fixate on it, to let it crush religious hope; yet I also believe that a religious faith will not be satisfactory to us unless we feel that it has faced up to the number and horror of natural evils, such as cancer and earthquakes, and to the depth of the human capacity for evil, such as cruelty, exploitation, and deceit. It seems that for some people, religion comes to mind only when they find themselves in a crisis situation. As a popular saying puts it, "There are no atheists in foxholes." I doubt that that's perfectly true, but I would be willing to bet that there are *fewer* atheists in foxholes! We need not restrict our discussion to the battlefront, however, for there are numerous "foxhole situations" in life: a student failing out of school; a student graduating from school without the least idea of what to do with the rest of her life; a marriage falling apart; a sole supporter of his family losing his job. Clearly, a religion worth having is going to be a religion that has fathomed the frightening waters of life and found a solid foundation beneath them. A "fair-weather religion" is one of the most useless things I can think of. It's like carrying around an umbrella that has no covering: when you really need it, it is of no use to you!

Now I don't want you to think that I am encouraging a "foxhole" type of religion only. Whitehead, again, has suggested what needs to be said.[12] Namely, our religion should be capable of functioning at all temperatures and in all climates—and that includes those "below-zero" temperatures when the callousness of some human beings or the indifference of nature makes the human adventure seem a painful and meaningless accident. A healthy religion, then, will be one that is helpful in adversity and prosperity, that augments the beauty of the good times and helps us get through the bad times. It will be one in which our deity stands at the *center* of our everyday life as well as at its *periphery,* during those extraordinary moments of great fortune, misfortune, or decision.

## OPTIMISTIC

A fifth trait of a healthy religion, and the final trait we shall discuss, is that it is *optimistic.* You might say, "Yes, but it is optimism based on escape from reality!" Some even say, "Religion is a crutch." To be sure, religion has served as an escapist crutch in all three senses in which my students have interpreted that saying: (1) religion, like alcohol, drugs, sex, etc., can be an escape from facing and coping with a serious problem, so that instead of acknowledging the facts and struggling with them, we hide ourselves from them with a veil of illusion or a cloak of pleasure; (2) rather than doing what is within our power to do, we can "lean" on the Lord to do it; (3) rather than accepting the responsibility for having done what we should not have done, we can blame it on the will of God. I agree that these are real and serious ways in which religion has been misused. There is yet another sense in which religion is a crutch, however, and it is a sense that calls for neither shame nor reproach. Why? Because when you're crippled, you need a crutch! And we are all crippled by the ambiguity of life: its meaning is not clear—all sorts of things *might* be the case, but none is clearly the case. Consequently, *we* have to choose *something* to stand on, something to give life unity, meaning and direction. You may choose the crutch (the religion) that was given to you as a child, but *you* now have to choose it for yourself. Having reached the age of self-conscious deliberation, you can no longer blame your parents and educators for what you believe. You are a free agent. If you continue to believe what they taught you, you must now add that it is because *you* are convinced that they knew best!

You may well decide that they were wrong, however, and where does that leave you? You can't simply divest yourself of all beliefs about reality and value, yet survive. Why? Because you'd be as helpless and dependent as a newborn infant. Hence, if you reject one set of beliefs, you are confronted with the necessity of replacing it with another set. We simply cannot get along without a crutch of some kind. It is as though we were born crippled and have to find or construct a crutch in order that we can get along in life. (The crutch parents and teachers start us off with quickly becomes such a part of us that we don't realize it is a crutch!)

Clearly the "crutch" I have been talking about consists of ideas that "bake no bread." That is, religious beliefs about the nature of reality and value are of no practical value in the narrow sense of the word "practical." You can't use religious beliefs to make better cars or grow larger crops. Such ideas are, in that sense, useless. Consequently, some pragmatists and Marxists contend that such ideas ought to be banned from discourse as a waste of time. To the contrary, I would like to say a few things in behalf of nonpractical ideas.

Beliefs that "bake no bread" can make a significant difference in our lives in terms of (1) the way we feel about ourselves and others, (2) how we bear up under tragedy, (3) how we persevere under adversity and temptation. What I am claiming is that what we *believe* has a reflexive influence upon our attitudes, feelings, and actions, even when we are aware that our belief is a matter of feeling or hope and not of knowledge or probability. Consider, for example, the following contradictory alternatives: (1) that you are to some extent a free agent, able to choose what you will do and able to choose to what extent you will persevere in doing what you choose; (2) that you are in every instance the puppet of forces beyond your control—unable to choose other than as you do and unable to stop other than when you do. To adopt a metaphor from Dostoyevsky, according to the second position, you are a piano upon which Nature and Society play. You have no more control over what you do than a piano has over the sounds it makes. The sounds it makes are determined by the keys that are struck, and the actions we emit are determined by the natural and social forces that play upon us. Now these alternative beliefs "bake no bread," yet you must believe one way or the other, and which way you believe, it seems to me, is going to have a distinctive impact upon your feelings toward your life, toward its worth, its possibilities, and its meaning. It should also have an impact upon how you feel about and relate to other persons. (Reconsider in this context the sentence the student wrote before committing suicide: "I'm going to die anyway." Also, how well does a condemned man enjoy his last meal, sumptuous though it be? Clearly, the context of beliefs within which we operate makes a difference in how we feel about things.)

Having defended the value of nonpractical beliefs, I now want to claim that a *healthy religion is a mode of creativity devoted to the construction (or appropriation), mainenance, and celebration of an optimistic theory of the origin, nature, and destiny of human being.*[13] This optimism may be grounded in the Lord, humanity, science, or something else. It may be magnificent or very modest, but it is always there; for in the final analysis, religion has nothing to do with cynicism. Indeed, the opposite of healthy religion is *nihilism:* the systematic denial that there is anything truly good or that there is any reason for hope. The healthy religious impulse asks, Inasmuch as our situation is ambiguous and uncertain, why take a hopeless view of our situation when we can take an optimistic one? Why believe something that takes the wind out of your sails? that takes the fight out of you? that leaves you depressed? Within the limits set by logic, science, and your own sense of realism, why not look at the world through that set of ideas which to you is conducive to the fullest enjoyment of existence? As Tennyson bids us in his poem, "The Ancient Sage," "Cleave ever to the sunnier side of doubt."

To be sure, all pessimists are not emotionally depressed. Miguel de Unamuno, Spanish author of *Tragic Sense of Life,* accuses the pessimist of being an arrogant snob![14] The pessimist Unamuno has in mind is a pessimist because it is stylish and because he thinks he knows beyond question what reality is really like! This kind of person clearly takes pleasure in his pessimism. I am concerned about those who do not. To them I recommend religion because I believe that religion at its best is a form of "creative insecurity."[15] A sensitive, alert person cannot escape altogether from insecurity, but it need not be crushing, and a healthy religion is committed to helping people cope with insecurity in creative, growth-enhancing ways. It is a matter of believing that which gives one the maximum of hope, of meaning, and of peak-experience without compromising intellectual integrity. To put it another way, religion as a mode of creativity is the construction or adoption of an interpretation of life that (1) is compatible with one's understanding of logic and fact, and (2) causes one to have a maximum of joy in being. A healthy religion doesn't oppress us but liberates us; it doesn't constrict us but releases our energies and enthusiasms; it doesn't leave us drifting but gives us direction. In order to do these things, clearly one's religion must wrestle with the problem of evil and put it into such a perspective that neither *evil* nor *indifference* is seen as the ultimate fact of existence. Why do I say this? Because I see no way to be the least bit optimistic if I become convinced that evil or indifference is the ultimate fact of reality. Again it seems to me that such a conviction must wash back over all of one's feelings toward life. Yes, people differ greatly with regard to how *much* they can hope for, but whenever the flame of hope goes out altogether, so does the heartbeat of religion.

In conclusion, without a frame of orientation that nurtures within us a deep and abiding hope, we are crippled indeed. So perhaps it is *without* a healthy religion that we need a crutch. Perhaps a healthy religious faith is our "natural" means of spiritual balance and vitality.

© 1960 United Feature Syndicate, Inc.

**Footnotes**

1. Paul Tillich, *Biblical Religion and the Search for Ultimate Reality* (Chicago: The University of Chicago Press, 1955), pp. 60–61. For an explanation of the four things Tillich says faith is not, see chap. 2, "What Faith Is Not," in Tillich's *Dynamics of Faith* (New York: Harper & Brothers, 1957).

2. Ibid., chap. 1, Sec. 5.

3. Friedrich von Hügel, *Essays and Addresses on the Philosophy of Religion,* quoted in John H. Hick's *Philosophy of Religion,* 2nd ed. (Englewood Cliffs, N.J.: Prentice-Hall, Inc., 1973), p. 71.

4. For a recent analysis of paradox in both science and religion by a physicist-philosopher, see Ian Barbour's *Myths, Models, and Paradigms* (New York: Harper & Row, Publishers, 1974).

5. John Henry Cardinal Newman, *Apologia Pro Vita Sua* (New York: The Modern Library, 1950), p. 182.

6. Ibid., pp. 237–238. You might want to say to Cardinal Newman, "Okay, I'll accept your contention that 10,000 difficulties do not make a doubt. But what about 10,001? or 10,002? Surely at *some* point difficulties legitimately cause doubt!" For a brief and provocative statement of this kind of reaction to Newman's point, see Antony Flew's "Theology and Falsification," in *New Essays in Philosophical Theology,* Antony Flew and Alasdair MacIntyre, eds. (New York: The Macmillan Company, 1955).

7. *The Mystery of Being,* 2 vols., Gabriel Marcel (Chicago: Henry Regnery Company, 1960). The religious existentialist philosopher gives an illuminating discussion of the difference between a "problem" and a "mystery." For a brief introduction to Marcel, see *Gabriel Marcel,* by Sam Keen (Richmond, Va.: John Knox Press, 1967).

8. Alfred North Whitehead, *Religion in the Making* (New York: World Publishing Co., 1973), p. 97.

9. Milton Steiberg, *Basic Judaism* (New York: Harcourt, Brace & World, Inc., 1947). 172 pages. Very readable.

10. For the writings of Marx himself, and his colleague, Friedrich Engels, see *On Religion* (New York: Schocken Books, Inc., 1964). For a brief introduction to Marx's position, see *Religion and Atheism* by William Luijpen and Henry Koren (Pittsburgh: Duquesne University Press, 1971).

11. See "Religion: Opiate or Inspiration of Civil Rights Militancy among Negroes?" by Gary T. Marx, for a sociologist's investigation of this question. Reprinted several places, including *Religion in Sociological Perspective,* Charles Y. Glock, ed. (Belmont, Calif.: Wadsworth Publishing Co., Inc., 1973).

12. Whitehead, *Religion in the Making,* pp. 53–54.

13. I make this distinction between "construction" and "appropriation" of a religious faith in order to allow for both the *naturalist,* who believes that religious faith is the product of human experience and reflection, and those *theists* who believe that given the limitations and perversities of the human mind, no religion is worth our time save one that has been revealed by a supreme being—and it, having been revealed by a supreme being, should not

be altered but accepted whole. Karl Barth represents the theistic position and John Dewey the naturalistic position. John Hick, contemporary philosopher of religion, believes, like Barth, that there is a God who reveals Himself to us, but Hick believes also that God reveals Himself in such a way that we are forced to *interpret* what He is saying. See chap. iv, "Revelation and Faith," of Hick's *Philosophy of Religion,* 2nd ed. (Englewood Cliffs, N.J.: Prentice-Hall, Inc., 1973).

14. See Miguel de Unamuno, *Tragic Sense of Life* (New York: Dover Publications, Inc., 1954), p. 326.

15. Peter Bertocci develops this idea in his book, *Religion as Creative Insecurity* (New York: Association Press, 1959).

# Attitudes toward
# Religious Propositions

- What are four attitudes a person may have toward religious propositions?
- How do the rationalist and the antirationalist disagree regarding the power and scope of human reason?
- Using a "hope" interpretation of faith, how can the proposition, "I believe in God" be related to both the present and the future?
- In what sense do religious propositions have an aesthetic function in human life?
- What are the relations of mature religious faith to *doubt* and to *courage?*
- In what ways is the mature religious person "open" and why?
- What is the mature religious person endeavoring to discover, and what are the two passions that drive her or him?
- What is the significance of "faith as hope" for interreligious dialogue?
- What are three noetic perversions of religious faith? Explain them.

Many persons believe that to have a religious faith means to be certain that what you believe is true. This attitude toward one's religious beliefs has caused a great deal of conflict in the past as groups with mutually exclusive faiths have encountered one another, each claiming to be the one true religion. Today that attitude is not causing *conflict* so much as it is causing *doubt*. Why? Because an increasing number of people are asking: "Since I am not *certain* about the nature of reality and value, how can I have a religious faith at all?" Given their assumption that religious faith is a matter of being certain, these people understandably believe that they must reject religious faith. What we shall see in this chapter is that such rejection may not be necessary. Why? Because there are at least four basic attitudes one can take toward one's religious faith, and only one of them is dogmatic. We shall call these four attitudes *knowledge, belief, faith,* and *hope*. In ordinary language there is considerable overlap among the meanings of these four terms, and some of them are used interchangeably. As a consequence, discussions about belief and faith are often confusing, because it's not clear to all parties how these terms are being used. Hence, what I propose to do is to give a narrower, more precise meaning to each term than it has in ordinary discourse. This should bring greater clarity into our thinking and talking about religious credence by providing us with four distinct forms of it, together with a different term for each form. Sometimes, however, because of your own ways of using these terms, you may feel uncomfortable with the meanings to which I restrict them. I do too, at times. Still, by restricting them as I do I am able to bring out four clear attitudes toward the truth of a proposition, and that, for our purposes, seems worth the discomfort. Further, as long as we stay with ordinary language, rather than inventing new terms (and how could we define new religious terms apart from ordinary language?), uneasiness is inevitable because—for our purposes—we will be restricting terms with many meanings to only one of their meanings. Of course, my way of restricting them may cause more dissatisfaction than is necessary. Hence, if you're sufficiently unhappy, I encourage you to improve upon my own attempt to bring clarity into our understanding of the modes of religious adherence.


## FOUR BASIC ATTITUDES: KNOWLEDGE, BELIEF, FAITH, AND HOPE

As I have said, there are at least four basic attitudes you can take toward your religious beliefs. First, you can hold that your religious beliefs are *absolutely and demonstrably true*. This would mean that you are not only convinced beyond a doubt in your own mind that your religious beliefs are true, but that you are also convinced that their truth is *demonstrable* to anyone who is intelligent enough and unbiased enough to follow your presentation of the evidence. Here, then, we have "rational certainty." You claim that your religion is based on knowledge, on the certainty of proof. The Roman Catholic Church, for example, holds that the existence of God can be proved in this manner (though it does not hold that all of its doctrines can be proved by reason). In the thirteenth century A.D., St. Thomas Aquinas provided five such proofs of the existence of God (see his *Summa Theologica,* Part One, Question Two, Third Article), and in 1940, Pope Pius XII asserted, in his encyclical, *Humani Generis,* "Human reason can, without the help of divine revelation and grace, prove the existence of a personal God by arguments drawn from created things [that is to say, drawn from the way the world is]." Hence, Pius XII is claiming that one who can and does follow such arguments as those of Aquinas will come to *know* that there is a personal God.

There are other possible attitudes toward the doctrines of religion, however. You might hold that though you do not think that the doctrines of your religion can be proved to be true beyond a doubt, still you believe they are *the most plausible explanation of the nature of reality.* In other words, *given the evidence presently at hand,* you believe that your religion is more likely the true explanation of reality than any other explanation with which you are familiar. This is the kind of position taken by F. R. Tennant in his two-volume work, *Philosophical Theology* (see bibliography). Here we have *empirical confidence,* of one degree or another, rather than *rational certainty.* Instead of saying that you *know* the claims of your religion are true, you say that you *believe* they are true, and your belief is based on *evidence* which doesn't *prove* your religion is true, but which, in your judgment, gives it a higher *probability* of being true than any other explanation enjoys. However, the fact that your commitment is based on evidence means that should old evidence be discredited, new evidence be discovered, or a more convincing analysis of the evidence be arrived at, then the strength of your belief should fluctuate appropriately, and if your present religion is in your own judgment surpassed on the probability scale by some new explanation of reality, then your allegiance should switch immediately to the new explanation—since your implicit objective is to be always committed to that explanation of reality which enjoys the highest probability of being true. This attitude is captured very nicely in a statement by James Cornman and Keith Lehrer in their *Philosophical Problems and Arguments.* They write regarding the question of the existence of God: "Although God may exist, as evidence unavailable to human beings might indeed show, the conclusion that we as rational beings should draw, based on the evidence discussed in this chapter, is that God does not exist. . . ."[1] Note Cornman and Lehrer's assumption that *as rational beings* we should ever make sure that we believe only those propositions which have the highest likelihood of being true, regardless of our hopes and intuitions.

Yet is the concept of probability even *applicable* to the question of the truth or falsity of a world-view? Some religious persons are unable to say that they *believe* their religion is true, much less that they *know* it is true, because they believe that it is *impossible* (either for practical or theoretical reasons) to establish the various truth probabilities of the different world views. John Hick, for example, is himself a believer in the Christian God, yet he discredits probabilistic arguments to the existence of God by arguing that the concept of probability cannot be applied legitimately to the question of the existence of a unique infinite being, such as God.[2]

Whether Hick is correct or not, one may be convinced that he does not *know* that his religion is true, and he may think it would be inaccurate to say that he *believes* that his religion is true, yet he may have *faith* that his religion is true. What does it mean to have faith that something is true? It means to have the *feelings* of confidence which normally accompany *knowledge,* but with regard to propositions about which you are neither rationally certain nor empirically confident, since you do not believe that you have either reasons which prove them true or evidence which shows that they are probably true. You do, however, have a feeling of *emotional confidence* that these propositions are true. You have the feeling of certainty without the grounds of certainty, and this, it seems to me, is yet a third type of attitude one may have toward one's religion. This kind of faith, it should be noted, is not the result of an exertion of will or of a process of reasoning; it is simply the way one's feelings are constituted at the moment. Some persons, such as Karl Barth and Miguel Unamuno, would say that it is "a gift of grace." Unamuno writes in *The Agony of Christianity* that faith "issues from grace and not from arbitrary choice. He who has merely a craving for faith does not have faith."[3] Faith is received, not achieved. Better yet: it happens.

Fourth, and finally, you may not be able to say in honesty about a religion that you know it is true, or that you believe it is true, or even that you have faith that it is true. Still, you might *hope* that it is true, for it may represent to you the most attractive interpretation of reality of which you are aware. Hence, in expressing your commitment to that religion, you would not be claiming it to be true on logical or empirical grounds; nor would you be claiming to feel as though it is true. You would be claiming only that you *hope* it is true and that you believe that there is a *possibility* that it is true. (It would be irrational to hope that it is true if you believe that there is no possibility that it is true, but it would not be irrational to hope that it is true if you believe that there is the least possibility that it is true, regardless of how improbable it might seem.) Miguel de Unamuno is the exemplar *par excellence* of this fourth position. See his *Tragic Sense of Life,* wherein he insists that "with reason or without reason or against reason" he will persist in his hope that there is life after death.[4]

These attitudes and their descriptions can be outlined as follows:

Knowledge: Rational Certainty: Based on proof

Belief: Empirical Confidence: Based on probability

. . . . . . . . . . . . . . . . . . . . . . . . . . . . . . . . . . . . . . . . . . . . . . . . . . . . . . . . .

Faith: Emotional Confidence: Based on feeling

Hope: Emotional Desire: Based on attractiveness

The dotted line points to the question of the power and scope of human reason. "Knowledge" and "Belief" assume that human reason can discern the ultimate nature of reality. "Faith" and "Hope" do not. To be sure, we would like to *be convinced* by reasons or evidence that certain claims about the nature of reality are true, and we would like to *feel* that they are true. Hence, from this perspective hope is the least satisfactory of these four positions, and faith the next to least satisfactory, since hope by itself is backed by neither argument nor feeling, and faith by itself is backed by only one of these. But perhaps hope and faith are the best we can do. Perhaps it is impossible to resolve the question of the nature of reality by means of human reason. Let's take a look at two positions, pro and con.

On the one extreme, there is a tradition of thinkers called *rationalists* who believe that reality is essentially transparent to the searching light of reason. It is as though reality were a large but transparent glass ball and human reason a powerful flashlight capable of illuminating every aspect of that ball. In principle, then, the rationalist believes that there is no height or depth or area of reality that cannot be fathomed by human reason. One of the most famous rationalists, G. W. F. Hegel, a nineteenth-century German philosopher, made this position quite clear in his inaugural address at the University of Heidelberg:

> Man, because he is mind, should and must deem himself worthy of the highest; he cannot think too highly of the greatness and power of his mind, and, with this belief, nothing will be so difficult and hard that it will not reveal itself to him. The being of the universe, at first hidden and concealed, has no power which can offer resistance to the search for knowledge; it has to lay itself open before the seeker—to set before his eyes and give for his enjoyment, its riches and its depths.[5]

Clearly Hegel believes that, in principle, human reason is able to answer with certainty the question of the nature of reality.

There are others, however, who believe that reality is not transparent to reason. These persons, let us call them *anti-rationalists,* believe that whereas reason is a very valuable tool, it is also a very limited tool. It can, for example, (1) do mathematics, (2) figure probabilities, (3) aid in the discovery of natural laws, and (4) check arguments for consistency. But it is *not a metaphysical flashlight* that can disclose ultimate truths about reality. Rather, as Søren Kierkegaard, a nineteenth-century Danish philosopher, put it, when it comes to questions about the nature of reality, human reason is like a judge who listens to all the evidence in a case, but then is missing from the bench when it's time for him to give a verdict! The point is that no matter how long or deeply we investigate questions about the nature of reality, we shall never find that THE answer is given to us. Rather, reality is always presented to us *ambiguously*—open to various interpretations, none of which is clearly true—all of which fit the data, but none of which fits it perfectly. To be sure, given your individual background (culture, family, etc.) and your present values, you will find some interpretations of reality *easier* to believe in than others. But upon philosophical analysis you will find, according to Kierkegaard, that you cannot demonstrate according to some universally accepted criteria that your interpretation is definitely true, or even more likely true than any other. Hence, your commitment must really be a matter of faith or hope.

Who is right in the debate between the rationalists and the anti-rationalists? I've already given myself away as some kind of a rationalist. But the debate is far too inconclusive for solemn pronouncements of "correct" and "incorrect." It is more important for you to figure out where your own sympathies lie, with the rationalists or the anti-rationalists, for that will help you get a perspective on how to react to a whole raft of issues, such as whether or not to take seriously arguments for the existence of God. Meanwhile, having briefly gone over each of these four attitudes towards one's religion, now let's turn around and work our way back through them, going in the other direction and giving special attention to their epistemological relations to one another and to how they might be combined.

The simplest form of religious engagement, epistemologically, is *hope:* the hope of sheer aspiration, with no ground other than desire, or the hope of sheer desperation, with nowhere else to turn. I am speaking, for example, of the sudden hope of the unbeliever that there is a God who will vindicate justice and mercy or the hope of a distraught mother that her child will live again. Such hope, I believe, is genuinely religious and need not, in order to be considered religious, be bolstered by a feeling that it is true or by evidence that it is true. Here we have the religious attitude in its simplest, least rationalized, least assuming form. Religiousness at this level is not a matter of knowing that a particular interpretation of reality is true, or of thinking that "given the evidence it is probably true," or of feeling that it is true, but simply of hoping that it is true because it is the best that one can imagine about reality.

When one's religious adherence is self-consciously understood to be a matter of hope, the articles of one's "faith" perform a kind of aesthetic function. For the sake of enhancing the felt quality of our lives we decorate the interior of our homes with attractive physical objects: paintings, sculpture, plants, music, etc. In like manner we can decorate the interior of our minds with attractive propositions—not without regard for their truth or falsity, but with primary regard for the quality of their impact on our lives. This aesthetic function of religion in our lives extends to religious symbols and rituals as well as to religious propositions. Hence, a religion can make a valuable contribution to one's life apart from any determination of its truth or falsity. This is especially important to note, inasmuch as religious doctrines are usually *beyond* the pale of verification anyway. When we do not have certainty, we must act on probability, and when we do not have even probability, what better than to act on our own deepest vision of the good?

Religious allegiance becomes more complex when one's hope is accompanied by emotional experiences or feelings which give one the confidence that what one hopes is true. Such confidence *happens* to us, we know not why—though we may believe that it is "a gift of grace." To be sure, you may not think that hope is involved in your faith, and it may not have been consciously present in your religious development. But if your faith is a healthy faith, then I believe that under questioning you would conclude that even if you lost your feeling of *confidence* that things are as you feel they are, you would continue to *hope* that they are that way. Hope, I am suggesting, implicitly undergirds faith. A person, for example, who under the onslaught of criticisms loses his confidence that there is a loving, omnipotent God, may nonetheless continue to hope that there is and that the criticisms can somehow be reconciled with God's love and omnipotence by means of His wisdom and our finitude.

Regarding the relations of faith and knowledge, it is easy to confuse the two with one another because of the feeling of certainty common to both. One of my students wrote in a paper that she "knew" that she was saved and that God had forgiven her sins. I asked her in what sense she was claiming to "know" these things. How, I asked, can you *know* something like this? She replied as follows:

> To answer that question I would like to define "faith." The best way I know of to do this is to tell you a story.
>
> "A minister had a son about eight years old. One day the son asked his father, 'What is faith, Daddy?' The father answered by taking the boy into his study and perching him up on the highest bookshelf in the room. He then asked his son, 'If you were to fall or jump down from there, do you think I would catch you?' The little boy was quick to answer, 'Sure, you'd catch me!' The father asked his son again, just to make certain, and the boy was just as confident in his reply. The father then demanded that the boy jump. The boy hesitated a moment and then jumped into his father's outstretched arms."

The student continued:

> This story communicates, to me anyway, what faith is all about. My "knowledge" of God's love is similar to the little boy's implicit trust in his father. I have *extreme* confidence that God is there and that I have salvation through Christ. There is always the possibility that the father would slip and

the boy fall to the floor. But the boy had to take his father on faith that he wouldn't slip that one time. So faith involves "knowledge." The boy had *no doubt* that his father would catch him and I have no doubts that God exists, that God is loving, and that God has forgiven my sins. I *know* no other way of putting it!

This is a beautiful example, it seems to me, of that attitude toward religious propositions which we have called "faith" rather than "knowledge." Clearly, "trust without doubt" is not the same thing as "knowledge," or even "belief." We can have a feeling of absolute confidence in someone and nonetheless be "let down" by them. Hence, to have such a feeling about someone's trustworthiness is not to *know* that they are trustworthy, even if they have been dependable in the past. A problem with confusing knowledge with faith is that it gives us the feeling of knowing something which we do not know. Presumably, *to know* that something is true involves the following: (1) it is true (since you can't know what is not true); (2) you have evidence or reasons that it is true; (3) your evidence or reasons mean that it is true (since if they didn't, then you might achieve the probability of belief, but not the certainty of knowledge); and (4) you are *aware* that your evidence or reasons mean that the proposition concerned is true (there is the possibility that you might not have realized the significance of the evidence or reasons which you have). But we have said already that faith is not *based* on evidence at all. Hence, it cannot be a form of knowledge, though it might be that faith can be reinforced by evidence. The confusion of faith with knowledge most likely occurs because a person takes his *feeling of certainty* about a proposition to be *conclusive evidence* that the proposition is true. Whereas, of course, how one *feels* about the truth of a proposition is usually irrelevant to the task of establishing its truth or falsity.[6]

Religious allegiance achieves a third level of complexity when one believes that one's hope or faith is supported by evidence which makes it seem more likely that it is true. Some people, for example, believe that religious experience itself is evidence in favor of the existence of God. Father Frederick Copleston, Jesuit priest and author of a widely used, multivolumed history of philosophy, made this point in a radio debate with Bertrand Russell, one of this century's most articulate critics of theism. "I don't regard religious experience as a strict proof of the existence of God," Copleston stated, "but I think it's true to say that the best explanation of it is the existence of God."[7] Other people emphasize order, purpose, beauty, and morality as lending credence to the idea that there is a personal God. Whether religious devotion can be confirmed legitimately by evidences of these sorts is, as we have seen, a question that is vigorously debated by philosophers and theologians. Whatever the correct answer, I believe it is fair to say that we would *prefer* that our religious allegiance be based not only on hope or faith but also on something which gives us a degree of *reasoned confidence* in what we are committed to. Without that objective basis of evidence, we feel all the more vulnerable to critics and the vacillations of our own feelings. With that support, there is a kind of security which we do not enjoy otherwise. Hence, it is understandable that many people whose commitment is of the nature of hope or faith work hard at trying to find reasons and evidence which protect their commitment from external critics and internal moods.

Still, even hope confirmed by faith and evidence is not identical with knowledge, in the sense defined earlier. Nor am I optimistic that we ever can achieve knowledge of the truth of any set of basic religious doctrines. To be sure, we *want* knowledge that *x* (our religion) is true, rather than having to settle for hope or faith that it is true. For that very reason we must be careful to avoid premature closure of the gap between our evidence and our convictions.[8] Or, to put it another way, we should not allow ourselves to be deceived into thinking that the nature of the closure between our evidence and our feelings is of the nature of knowledge or belief when it isn't. Neither knowledge nor belief in any legitimate sense can be achieved by allowing a feeling of certainty to replace a lack of evidence. To be sure, the believer may not be aware of what has happened. He is convinced that he *knows* that his religion is true! But if he can be led through the land of philosophical distinctions, I believe he will see that we must make a distinction between what we *feel*, what we *believe*, and what we *know*, and having made those distinctions, I believe we can convince him that his devotion is not based on knowledge but on hope or faith, perhaps reinforced by belief. Let's pursue this line of thought a bit further.

Clearly, feeling that a religious belief is true is not equivalent to knowing that it is true. If that were the case, then Judaism, Christianity, Islam, Hinduism, and Buddhism would all be true, since they each have devotees who feel that their religion is true. But they cannot all be true, since if, for example, the creed of Islam is true, then Judaism and Christianity are false at crucial points. Hence, feeling that a religion is true cannot be accepted as sufficient evidence that it is true. Moreover, I am convinced presently that it is in principle impossible to prove conclusively the truth of any religious faith.[9]

I would not deny that some things relevant to religious faith can be known by means of reasons. I am, for example, convinced that there is something which is uncreated, eternal, and indestructible. The argument goes as follows: (1) something cannot come from nothing; (2) if anything exists, then there is something which cannot become nothing; (3) something exists (at the very least, I exist while I am thinking through this argument). From these premises it can be concluded, I believe, that there is something which has always existed and will always exist. Whether that something is matter, the Lord, or something else is a question we won't go into here. The important point at the moment, if I am correct about the soundness of the argument, is the religious poverty of the conclusion. Indeed, all the conclusions, of which I am convinced by metaphysical reasoning, are far from religiously adequate and are compatible with a number of more in-clusive theories that are mutually exclusive. Simply because something is uncreated, imperishable, and indestructible does not mean it is worthy of worship, and even if we all agree that the foundation of reality, whatever it is, is uncreated and indestructible, still we cannot by metaphysical reason-ing, as far as I can see, determine whether that "ground of being" is mind-less or intelligent, favorably disposed toward humans or indifferent. Further, there seems to be no conclusive means of settling the question of human destiny for we can never *know* that our state of affairs has reached a point of eternal fixity. Even if we die and come back to consciousness in an unearthly paradise, how can we know then that we won't die again, and this time without a return of consciousness? Or, how can we know that our paradise won't turn into a nightmare? John Hick argues that "continued personal existence after death" in a paradisal kingdom such as is described in the Bible would provide "a religiously unambiguous" verification of the Judaic-Christian faith in life after death.[10] I have to disagree because as long as the future is before us—and that, I think, is where it shall always be—our situation is ambiguous no matter how completely we might be lulled by repetition into thinking otherwise. We could learn a lesson here from Ber-trand Russell's chicken. Russell tells (with a bit of embellishment from me) of a farmer who had a chicken that he raised from the egg. Every day the farmer religiously fed the chicken at the same time and place. The chicken, never having experienced anything else, understandably expected that whenever the farmer appeared at the special time and place, it would be fed. Imagine the poor bird's surprise when one day instead of getting its stomach fed, it got its neck wrung. Such a touching tale, I fear, would haunt me even inside the pearly gates. But, if I make it, perhaps Hick will be there to reassure me.[11]

Finally, in this attempt to show some of the severe difficulties that encounter any attempt to prove a religious doctrine, I would like to say something about the practice of presuming to prove a doctrine by referring it to the authority of a sacred book or a sacred person. This, it seems to me, does not provide us with a resting place at all. It only raises the question of how we might become convinced that the book or that person speaks the truth. Here, too, I cannot conceive how we can achieve knowledge that a certain book or person *always* speaks the truth. There are, however, people such as my friend, Reverend Herman Eckelmann, an electrical engineer as well as a minister, and Professor Robert C. Newman, Ph.D. in astrophysics from Cornell University, now at the Biblical School of Theology, who believe that though we cannot achieve absolute intellectual certainty in either religion *or science,* that still in religion, as well as science, we can achieve, "that level of certainty which we can attain in everyday activities and decisions and by which we would be held accountable in court, in the

army, by our employer, or by our friends.''[12] This strikes me as an interesting approach, worthy of serious consideration. Presumably this *principle
of accountability* should be applied to every religion and then one becomes
"morally responsible" for following that religion which exhibits "that level
of certainty" for which we are held accountable in everyday life. Clearly,
there will be difficulties if one concludes that no religion exhibits that
degree of certainty or that two or more religions exhibit it to an equal extent.
For an application of the principle to Christianity, see *Science Speaks,* by
mathematician Peter Stoner, who was assisted by Newman. Meanwhile,
let's return to our analysis of the difference between knowledge and faith.

A person who is philosophically sound, I believe, will realize that the
movement from his feelings, experiences, and thinking, to the conclusion,
let us say, that the Lord God exists, is a movement which involves "a leap
of faith"—a leap which is taken because the leaper hopes that the Lord is
real. A believer might object, "Look, I *know* that it was when I went to the
altar and accepted Jesus that a change came into my life"—meaning: "I
know Jesus is real because I felt him come into my life and I have seen the
changes He has made." I agree that we must not deny the spiritual efficacy
of a certain kind of context and of certain actions (such as being in a revival
service, walking to the altar, etc.), but to admit the spiritual efficacy of such
a setting and such acts for some persons is not to prove that the feelings and
changes which ensued were brought about by a risen Christ. To repeat,
that kind of argument would also "prove" the truth of Indian religions, of
Islam, of paganism, etc. If one is *philosophically rigorous,* one is reduced
to acknowledging what was done, what happened, and that one *hopes* or
has faith that the changes which occurred were really brought about by the
Great Spirit, or Jesus, or Allah, or whomever. But that is something we
cannot know—any more than we can know that there are minds other than
our own. We certainly hope there are, but we cannot know that there are.
We never see directly another person's mind, his feelings or thoughts; we
assume them. And when we become aware of the possibility that there *are*
no other minds, but only other bodies, we hope that that is not the case.
We hope that we are loved in feeling as well as in behavior.

This last point raises the interesting question of the relation of hope to
time. Ordinarily we think of hope in relation to the future only, but it also
has important relations to the present and the past. Regarding the past, one
might hope, for example, that one's carelessness did not contribute causally
to a friend's accidental death or that Jesus really did die for the sins of man
or that the Koran really was dictated to Mohammed by Allah. With regard
to the *present,* one might hope that the feeling of a divine presence is due to
the real presence of a personal, supreme being and not to a chemical
imbalance in the body or to a self-stimulated illusion. Also, one might hope
that one's present behavior is not simply and solely a function of the past
(recall our discussion of determinism in Chapter 5), and that one's suffering
is serving a cause which is *genuinely worthy* and not simply a matter of

personal whim. Regarding the future, one might hope that lives cut short by tragedy will be restored to growth and that loved ones will be brought together again. In spite of the unusualness of relating hope to the past and the present, all three relations appear to be present in Hebrews 11:1 (New Testament): "Faith," it is written, "is the assurance of things hoped for, the conviction of things not seen." "Assurance" refers to that feeling of confidence which is the key element of "faith," as we defined it earlier. "Things hoped for" can be, as we just noted, past as well as future. A Christian, for example, might hope that his sins *were* really forgiven when he repented five years ago and that he *will* be granted eternal life in heaven after death. "The conviction of things not seen" can be read to mean *confidence* that things *in the present* are a certain way even though we do not *know* that they are. A good example here is the confidence of an Orthodox Jew that his experience of the presence of God is the result of the presence of God, rather than simply of electrochemical processes in his body. Again, our experience calls for interpretation, and even when we are not confident on grounds of reason that things are a certain way, still we may hope that they are. "For now," as St. Paul puts it, "we see through a glass darkly."[13]

To review briefly, there may be in a person's religious development a point before which he believes that his commitment is a matter of knowledge because he finds either (1) the evidence or (2) his experience to be compelling. When he reaches the point, if ever, at which he realizes the inconclusiveness of the evidence and the *alternate ways* of explaining his experiences, he realizes that his adherence is not based on knowledge. Neither, I suspect, is it ever *only* a matter of belief, for one can react to a probable proposition—including "God exists"—with enthusiasm, indifference, or aversion. If a fundamental religious proposition is greeted with enthusiasm, it is because one hopes it is true. Hence, philosophy ultimately gives religion back to us, but it gives it back in the form of hope rather than knowledge. We can *hope* that something is true and *act* as though it is true without thinking that we *know* it is true and without *believing* it is true. We can persist in our hope even when it is not accompanied by encouraging experiences and arguments, though I believe such hope will motivate us to defend and strengthen it in whatever ways we can. At the very least, I believe religious hope will employ reason to assure itself that what it hopes is a meaningful possibility. If more is possible, then blessed are those whose hopes *are* confirmed by feeling, reason, and action. Therein we have religious conviction in its richest form.

## FAITH, DOUBT, AND COURAGE

If the mature religious person realizes that his commitment is based on hope and not knowledge, then Paul Tillich is correct, it seems to me, in saying that doubt will be *included* in a mature religious faith as a structural feature of it. Why? Because at the same time a person feels that he is in the presence of that which is worthy of his absolute commitment, he is also capable of realizing that he is *fallible* and therefore may be wrong—no matter what or who it is to which he is drawn, whether it be Marxism or Hinduism. It is not true, then, as one of my students claimed, that religious faith "ends having to worry about explanations." Indeed, the severe loss of self-confidence into which one can be plunged by the twists and turns of the religious venture are highlighted well in the career and reflections of Cardinal John Newman. Reared in the Church of England, he became a priest in the same and was convinced absolutely that the pope of the Catholic Church was the Anti-Christ. Gradually, however, after years of debate, discussion, correspondence, and reading, Newman began to lose confidence in the soundness of the Church of England and felt a growing conviction that, horror of horrors, the Catholic Church is what it claims to be—namely, the one true church. Newman was distraught by the demise of one absolute conviction, regarding the orthodoxy of the Church of England, and he was troubled by the emergence of another, regarding the Church of Rome. How, he asked himself, "was I any more to have absolute confidence in myself? how was I to have confidence in my present confidence? how was I to be sure that I should always think as I thought now?"[14] In the light of his intellectual conclusions regarding the Church of Rome, he felt it was his duty to convert, but at the same time he was fearful of becoming victimized again by illusion. "I had been deceived greatly once," he wrote:

> how could I be sure that I was not deceived a second time? I then while in the Church of England thought myself right; how was I to be certain that I was right now? How many years had I thought myself sure of what I now rejected? how could I ever again have confidence in myself? To be certain is to know that one knows; what test had I, that I should not change again, after that I had become a Catholic?[15]

Having undergone this experience even once, we rightfully become apprehensive about further changes of commitment, and even about committing ourselves at all.[16]

Because of this awareness of our fallibility, Paul Tillich claims that a self-conscious religious faith is an act of courage, a daring affirmation of one's deepest hopes in spite of the fact that one realizes one might be wrong.[17] Hence, religious faith is a risk, and the mature believer realizes this. It does not follow, of course, that such a person, because he is aware that there might be something better than that to which he is presently committed, is continually wearing himself out seeking for that something. Sometimes, and perhaps most times, he doesn't feel the need for something better than he has. Moreover, he has a right to enjoy to the fullest the good that he has. But if he is asked about the nature of his commitment, he acknowledges that it is not a matter of knowledge and that now we "see through a glass darkly." Consequently, he remains open at all times to *criticisms* of his faith and to *alternatives* to his faith, for (1) he realizes that he is fallible and that his critics may therefore be correct, and (2) he wants to be committed to the *best* that there *is* and he realizes that, again owing to his fallibility, what he presently believes to be the best may not in fact be so.

The mature religious person also realizes that he would be foolish to reject the best that he knows before he has actually found something better to replace it. To adopt Cardinal Newman's expression, 10,000 difficulties do not warrant giving something up if you have nothing better to take its place. Failure to realize this has led many a person to give up his religion prematurely. A person would be equally foolish to close himself off from the possibility of discovering something better, if it does exist. Right? Still, we can understand the anxiety of Tertullian, one of the great figures in early Christianity, who wrote:

> But if we are bound to go on seeking as long as there is any possibility of finding, simply because so much has been taught by others as well, we shall be always seeking and never believing. What end will there be to seeking? What point of rest for belief? Where the fruition of finding? There will be no end . . . and I shall wish I had never begun to seek. . . .[18]

Many of us have had that very experience of wishing we had never begun to seek. We grow weary and discouraged. But my interpretation of that state of affairs is that it is the result of either (1) the fact that we have not yet found anything worthy of our wholehearted commitment, or (2) the fact that we have come across something that is worthy but we haven't understood that fact deeply enough. I sometimes share Tertullian's impatience with the person who will not, because he cannot, rest content with anything; yet that person is also a tragic figure whose life is an unresolved chord. Moreover, those persons are to be sympathized with who *are* eager and able to bring the search to an end, but who have not yet apprehended anything that enables them honestly to do so. The appropriate response to these people by those who *do* have a message is not to condemn them when they are not won over, but to search for ever more effective methods of getting across the beauty of the message.

Please permit a remark about one other type of person. Given the urgent, concrete problems of the world, instead of wearing oneself out with the search for something better, one might self-consciously desist from further search, hope that one's religion is true, admit one's inability to prove it, and plunge oneself into the concrete task of feeding the hungry, housing the homeless, healing the sick, and fighting injustice. As long as abstention from the philosophical task is for such a purpose and is accompanied by epistemological humility, it has my blessing (for whatever it's worth). But we must not reason, "Hey, I'm not looking around anymore—so I must've discovered the truth!'' Contentment with a position is not equivalent to knowledge of its truth. C. S. Peirce, founder of American pragmatism, once pointed out that thinking is a bit like scratching. That is, when we get an intellectual itch, we think in order to get rid of it. When the "itch" goes away, we stop thinking. But, of course, just because a certain way of thinking makes the itch go away does not mean that we've struck on the truth. Sometimes an error will remove an itch quicker than the truth! Hence, we should be very cautious about making inferences from our contentment with a position to its truth.[19]

Finally, let's consider whether religious devotion founded on hope is an escape from reality into the realm of imaginary wish fulfillment. Friedrich Nietzsche says of Plato, for example, that he was "a coward before reality," fleeing into a realm of utopian visions which he projected into another world.[20] Is that the nature of all religious commitment when it understands itself as hope? Not at all. In the first place, it is possible to be committed to a religion that is totally earthly; that is, one's hope can be in the possibilities of humanity and Nature. Second, those who believe that we shall live again may also believe that their faith has significance for the living of this life. For example, Mahatma Gandhi, a great religious spirit who helped lead India to independence from Britain, said in his autobiography that "those who say that religion has nothing to do with politics do not know what religion means."[21] Hence, rather than seeing religiousness as an escape from reality, we should see it as *an endeavor to see if experience does not confirm a hopeful interpretation of reality.* This is consistent with the fact that though the thoughtful religious person does not claim to *know* that his beliefs are true, he *is* concerned to *discover* the truth about reality. Hence, he is not willing to rest content with what he feels at the moment to be true. Rather, he risks his feelings to criticisms and further experience. Why? Because he is driven by two passions, not one. He is driven by (1) the desire to know the truth about reality, as well as by (2) the hope that the best that he can conceive about reality is true.

## INTERRELIGIOUS DIALOGUE

To summarize, I am suggesting that religious commitment is primarily a matter of hope and faith, rather than of belief or knowledge. This understanding of religious devotion provides, I believe, a fruitful context within which members of diverse religions can enter into genuine dialogue with one another. They will not be able to do that as long as each religion is thought by its believers to be demonstrably "the one true religion." On that assumption the members of a religion must perceive all unbelievers either as persons who have not yet had their eyes opened or as people who are being intentionally obtuse. Clearly, when adherents of different religious positions take these attitudes toward one another, there can be no dialogue. They can only talk *at* one another about religious matters. None can take seriously the claims of the other, for each is convinced already that he *knows* that his own religion is the true or the best in some objective sense. Hence, the other person's claims about the superiority of his religion must be false, and the overriding task of the speaker is to show the listener where he is wrong about his religion and why he, the speaker, is right about his own position.

I must confess that such carryings-on with such slender evidence seem to me most inappropriate. Perhaps one reason why religious arguments so often lead to uncharacteristically rude behavior is that each participant feels that he has sufficient objective evidence to convince anyone who will "really listen," whereas, in fact, no one has that kind of evidence. How do we explain this blind spot on the part of each participant? Perhaps in terms of the following principle: we are more easily persuaded of the truth of that which we want to be true than of that which we do not want to be true; hence, the body of evidence which is adequate to give a person who wants a position to be true the feeling that it is true and has been proved to be such, is not adequate to persuade someone who doesn't want that position to be true. When the body of evidence *is* sufficient proof that a position is true, then, of course, the second person is being obstinate; but when the body of evidence isn't sufficient, it is the first person who is being obstinate in insisting that the evidence *is* conclusive. Just what the strength of the evidence is, of course, is not something that can be determined apart from an examination of the evidence itself, and—if a *belief* claim is being made, rather than a claim of knowledge—apart from a comparison of that set of evidence to the sets of evidence set forth by other religions. My own position presently is that it is impossible to demonstrate conclusively the truth of any set of religious doctrines, and I'm not optimistic about the possibility of establishing the probabilities of religions relative to one another. Hence, I believe that the argument approach to nonbelievers is *misleading* to those who are convinced (since they too become victims of the illusion that the evidence is conclusive) and *disturbing* to those who are not (since they not only are thrown into self-doubt as to whether they have in fact failed to grasp the true strength of the argument, but are also sometimes, if they persist, accused implicitly or explicitly of being dull-witted, pig-headed, sinful, or some combination thereof).

If, however, persons understood their religious commitments to be a matter of a hopeful interpretation of reality, then, it seems to me, they would be free to take one another seriously and to listen appreciatively, for they would have no vested interest in proving one another wrong. Each would understand that unless the others had been touched by something which to them was beautiful, meaningful, enriching, and empowering, they would not be religiously serious at all. All could share their hopes and feelings with one another plus (insofar as they have them) their reasons for thinking that their hope or faith might be true. W. C. Smith suggests in this same spirit, "Might it not be that the next step in missions would necessarily be one where one religious group says to another, 'This is what we have seen of the truth, this is what God has done for us; tell us what you have seen, what God has done for you; and let us discuss it together'?"[22] In such a context, there would be no reason for anyone to become defensive, for the overriding interest of each person would be to share his own experience of the sacred as fully as he could and to be open to the possibility of an even greater experience—from whatever direction it might come. And surely it is primarily by means of human interchange that others learn the beauty of our religion and that we learn the beauty of theirs. Hence, such a context should enable persons to share the good which they have come to know through their religion and to continue their quest to be involved with that religion which can give their lives the greatest meaning, the finest quality, the clearest direction. That religion, of course, might not be the one held presently. Consequently, we should always perform the difficult task of *affirming* the best that we know while *holding ourselves open* to that which is better—whether the better be (1) further development in the direction we are already headed in or (2) conversion to a different direction altogether.

Such mutual openness involves the responsibility of being honest in our descriptions—not describing our religion in colors more bright or less than we have actually experienced. Conversely, we should be sincerely and genuinely open to the words of others, letting them wash over us in all of their brilliance and subtlety. This means, of course, that we, like Cardinal Newman, might find ourselves being powerfully attracted to a new religion. No serious student of religion is immune to this risk. The only escapes I can see are to avoid other religions altogether or to never really open ourselves to the beauty others see in them. And that, I submit, is not consistent with our desire to have the best there is.

Before leaving the topic, I must add as a counterbalance that it would be foolish to interpret religious commitment as a mode of hope, rather than of knowledge, merely in order to put all religions on the same level for the sake of dialogue. If a religion, or its fundamental doctrines, can be proved true or false, then they should be. But until it is demonstrated objectively that positive knowledge can be achieved about the ultimate matters with which religion is concerned, I shall hold on pragmatic grounds that humanity and the individual will be better served by an interpretation of religion based on hope and faith.

## NOETIC PERVERSIONS OF FAITH

As a conclusion to this section on "faith as hope," I would like to point out some of the unfortunate consequences that are likely to follow from the belief that religious conviction is a mode of knowledge. We shall call these consequences "noetic perversions" of religious conviction because the word "noetic" refers to affairs of the intellect. First there is the attitude of *dogmatism* referred to briefly in the preceding section. Dogmatism, I am convinced, is the attitude of those who cannot live with the ambiguity of human experience—or who don't see the ambiguity (and not seeing it may be a function of not wanting to see it). The dogmatist— whether theistic or atheistic—escapes from the anxiety of ambiguity into the comfortable feeling of noetic certainty—even when that feeling is not warranted. The dogmatic attitude is one in which a person has the feeling that his religion is true and provably so; yet he does not, in fact, have reasons or evidence whereby he can prove it, so he must either admit to himself that his religion is not provably true (which admission would dispel his dogmatism) or, as we noted earlier, he must think nasty things about those listeners who object that his argument is not a sufficient basis for commitment. (Though—and here comes the inevitable "on the other hand" of the philosopher—we must not rule out the possibility that the listener *has* in fact failed to grasp the true strength of the argument!)

A second noetic perversion is *exclusiveness*. As we noted earlier, if you believe that you know the truth, then you don't take seriously what the person says who disagrees with you; you only try to figure out how to convert him. If he proves impervious to your appeals and arguments, then you avoid him—which is what I mean by exclusiveness. This attitude is an obstruction to universal human fellowship and I think I can give a good example of it. I once went to a football game and sat next to a minister I knew. The minister introduced me to a couple of seminary students who had come with him. Without further ado, one of the students looked me in the eye, asked me if I believed in the blood atonement (a doctrine some Christians hold), and added that if I didn't, he would have nothing further to do with me. Personally, I didn't feel that losing his friendship would have been any great loss, but I was disturbed by his attitude. When creedal questions of this sort destroy fraternal feeling between persons (or prevent it from arising), I believe that persons have gotten their priorities tragically out of line. Mutual respect and affection are more important than creedal differences—which doesn't mean that beliefs are unimportant, but that we should learn to differ in love. "We sometimes forget," writes W. C. Smith,

> that this means arriving at a point where outsiders can trust us, as well as one where we can understand, respect, and honour them. It means also arriving at a point . . . where we can appreciate other men's values without losing our allegiance to our own. The world has little profit from that broadminded relativist who accepts the diversity of men's loyalties because he feels that no loyalties are ultimately valid, nothing is inherently worthwhile. Modern relativism is sophisticated cynicism—and is a devastating, not a constructive force.[23]

A healthy religion, as we noted earlier, has no place for cynicism. Nor has it a place for dogmatic exclusiveness.

The third and final noetic perversion I would like to mention is *coercion*—that is, the willingness to use propaganda or force to make people commit themselves, or at least say that they are committing themselves, to a certain religious position, whether it be theistic, such as Christianity, or atheistic, such as communism. This, in my opinion, is one of the most pathetic and harmful perversions of religious commitment. Religious devotion should be a matter of profound personal commitment based on deep experience and reflection. In its healthy form, it is the fruit of free and unforced growth. To try to force it is to have a misunderstanding of it to start with. It is not the kind of thing that can be forced. Furthermore, to attempt to bring about religious commitment by means of force or propaganda is to make the poor victim conclude that that is what religion is all about. No wonder some people hate religion and see it as a threat to human freedom. I join them! But what we mutually hate is a perversion of religion and not religion itself. It has its healthy forms. Indeed, one of my reasons for writing this book is that misunderstandings of the nature of religious commitment have led some people to be unloving, arrogant, dogmatic, propagandistic, and persecuting, and have led some of their victims, understandably, to become misguided enemies of the entire religious enterprise. If I am correct, however, that religious allegiance is ultimately based on hope or faith and as such must ever be humble epistemologically, then the religious person must never in the name of knowledge breach the command to love. As St. Paul put it in I Corinthians 8, we should reject knowledge that "puffs up" for love that "builds up." Further, though faith and hope are precious ingredients of human life, love is even greater than these. Hence, in the event of a conflict of love with faith or hope, we should never let love be the loser.[24]

© 1965 United Feature Syndicate, Inc.

## Footnotes

1. James W. Cornman and Keith Lehrer, *Philosophical Problems and Arguments,* 2nd ed. (New York: The Macmillan Company, 1974), p. 407.

2. See chap. 2, "Teleology and Probability," in John Hick's *Arguments for the Existence of God* (New York: Herder & Herder, 1971).

3. Miguel Unamuno, *The Agony of Christianity* (New York: Frederick Ungar Publishing Co., 1960), pp. 75–76.

4. Miguel Unamuno, *Tragic Sense of Life* (New York: Dover Publications, Inc., 1954), p. 130.

5. J. Glen Gray, ed., *G. W. F. Hegel on Art, Religion, Philosophy* (New York: Harper Torchbook, 1970), pp. 20–21.

6. The classic introduction to the question of the nature of knowledge is Plato's dialogue, *Theatetus*. For a recent discussion, see Edmund Gettier's "Is Justified True Belief Knowledge?" It appeared originally in *Analysis*, 23 (June 1963), 121–123, and has been reprinted in the Bobbs-Merrill Reprint Series (Phil.–85) together with four replies by other authors.

7. Included in *Classic and Contemporary Readings in the Philosophy of Religion*, 2nd ed. John Hick, ed. (Englewood Cliffs, N.J.: Prentice-Hall, Inc., 1970), p. 291.

8. I do believe that a person with faith only would prefer that his faith be backed by evidence, but it should be noted that faith, because it is not built up on evidence, is superior to belief in the sense that it is not subject to disruption by the influx of new and negative evidence. Etienne Gilson, distinguished scholar in the tradition of St. Thomas Aquinas, in his book, *The Elements of Christian Philosophy* (New York: Doubleday & Co., Inc., 1960), p. 58, puts the point this way:

> Now, on the one hand, faith is a type of knowledge inferior to understanding; as a mode of knowing, merely to believe is not as good as to understand. On the other hand, if we consider these two ways of knowing from the point of view of their certitude, faith is incomparably more certain than understanding.

His use of terms is not identical with ours, but you should be able to make the proper substitutions with little trouble. Gilson claims also that what a person holds originally on the ground of faith, he might later come to believe or to know. Still, Gilson adds, the intellectual belief in or knowledge of a doctrine lacks the warmth and personal depth of faith, so that faith in a doctrine remains important even once belief in it or knowledge of it has been achieved. See especially chaps. 1, 2, and 3 of *Elements*.

9. I have been especially influenced in this regard by the writings of John Hick (see his *Arguments for the Existence of God* and *Faith and Knowledge*, 2nd ed. [Ithaca, N.Y.: Cornell University Press, 1966], Parts I and III) and Karl Jaspers (see his *Way to Wisdom* [New Haven: Yale University Press, 1954]).

10. See Hick's *Philosophy of Religion*, 2nd ed., pp. 90–95.

11. Russell's fowl philosophy can be found in *The Basic Writings of Bertrand Russell*, Robert E. Egner and Lester E. Denonn, eds. (New York: Simon and Schuster, Inc., 1967), pp. 150–151.

12. Contained in a letter from Robert Newman.

13. I Corinthians 13:12; King James Version.

14. John Henry Cardinal Newman, *Apologia Pro Vita Sua* (New York: The Modern Library, 1950), p. 111.

15. Ibid., p. 230.

16. William James, American philosopher and psychologist, has a fascinating essay on this topic in which he distinguishes between (1) the person who fears being in error more than losing the truth and (2) the person who fears losing the truth more than being in error. The first person, consequently, is more

conservative and the second more adventurous. The first is less frequently in error, but the second is more likely to come by the truth. The entire essay, "The Will to Believe," is worth your while. If you don't have time for the entire essay, go directly to Section VII. Reprinted in numerous places, James' essay can be found together with other interesting papers in *The Will to Believe and Other Essays on Popular Philosophy* (New York: Dover Publications, Inc., 1956).

17. See his *Dynamics of Faith* (New York: Harper & Brothers, 1957), Chap. 6. For a much more comprehensive and difficult statement by Tillich, see his *The Courage to Be* (New Haven: Yale University Press, 1952).

18. *Early Latin Theology,* Vol. V: *The Library of Christian Classics,* trans. and ed. S. L. Greenslade (Philadelphia: The Westminster Press, 1956), p. 38.

19. Peirce's clear and interesting essay, "The Fixation of Belief," can be found in *Philosophical Writings of Peirce* (New York: Dover Publications, Inc., 1955).

20. Friedrich Nietzsche, *The Portable Nietzsche,* Walter Kaufmann, ed. (New York: The Viking Press, Inc., 1968), p. 599.

21. Mohandas K. Gandhi, *An Autobiography: The Story of My Experiments with Truth* (Boston: Beacon Press, 1957), p. 504.

22. Wilfred Cantwell Smith, "Comparative Religion; Whither—and Why?" in *The History of Religions,* Mircea Eliade and Joseph Kitagawa, eds. (Chicago: The University of Chicago Press, 1959).

23. _____, *The Faith of Other Men* (New York: The New American Library, 1963), p. 13.

24. For Paul's classic statement on love, see I Corinthians 13 (New Testament).

# Commitment
# Without Absolutes

QUESTIONS TO THINK ABOUT

- How can the concept of the absolute retain meaning and importance for us if we are convinced that we cannot *know* what is absolute?
- What is the difference between absolute commitment and tentative commitment?
- Why is it legitimate to say, "Buddha is unsurpassed" but not to say, "Buddha is unsurpassable"? (Relate your answer to the difference between a finite set of objects and an infinite set.)
- What provides us with guidance for our lives in the absence of absolute knowledge of what is right and true and good?

An important problem relevant to our discussion in Chapter 6 is opened up by Frederick Streng in his valuable little book, *Understanding Religious Man.* He writes:

The legacy of Western Enlightenment, freedom from absolute commitments, has provided the conditions for a situation often recognized today: a monotony of uncommitted lives.

The freedom attained by rejecting one value orientation does not necessarily mean freedom from the bondage of another value orientation that also turns out to be less than ultimate. To exchange one idol for another is not spiritual freedom. How one can avoid slipping into spiritual ignorance in the midst of one's highest spiritual efforts is a continuing religious problem.[1]

This statement occurs in the conclusion of Streng's book, so he pursues it no further. I agree, however, that it is an important problem, so I would like to pursue it a bit—especially because in the last chapter I rejected the possibility of religious knowledge. The problem, as I shall speak to it, is as follows: If we do not, and cannot, have *knowledge* that our religious commitments are true, how can we justify being committed to anything at all? After all, if we have no knowledge of absolutes, then we have no way of judging with certainty whether one thing is really better than another; and if this is the case, then must not an enlightened person remain uncommitted to anything or be equally committed to all things? More specifically, how can *religious* commitment be possible for a person who shares this era's rejection of absolutes?

First, I would claim, man's noetic situation is such that he can never know whether he is exchanging "one idol for another." We must reject the belief that we can know that something is religiously absolute. That does not mean that we must reject the concept of the absolute. We can still understand what it would mean for there to be absolute values and truths. Indeed, we can also understand that there might *be* absolute values and religious truths even if we cannot know for certain what they are. Our inability to know what is absolute means only that we must take a different attitude toward that which *impresses* us as being absolute and toward that which others *claim* to be absolute. Most obviously, we must not adopt an attitude of knowledge toward it. Yet *how,* you might ask, can the concept of the absolute retain any meaning for us after we foreswear all ability to determine what is absolute? I'm not sure that question can be answered. It may be that the concept of absoluteness is a simple concept which one either grasps or doesn't grasp. The concept of triangularity, by contrast, is a complex concept which can be built up from the concept of straight lines. But from what do we build the concept of absoluteness? Perhaps it can be explicated at least partially in terms of the concept of the unsurpassable. That is, from the experience of some things being surpassable—one runner being surpassed by another in a race, one color being surpassed by another in brightness—perhaps we construct the notion of there being something that not only *is not* surpassed but *cannot* be surpassed in some respect! We have all, I suspect, had the experience of feeling one value surpass another in a specific situation—e.g., while helping an acquaintance with a minor problem, we are apprised that our parents need emergency help. Hence, one value can surpass another in importance, and it is conceivable that there is a value than which none is more important. Similarly, we have all had the experience of replacing one proposition with another because we became convinced that whereas the replaced proposition was not completely false, neither was it as accurate or complete as its replacement. Hence, one proposition can be truer than another, and it is conceivable that there are propositions which are absolutely true—that is, to which no improvement in truth value can be made. Our problem, of course, is that even though we can understand in these terms what it means if a proposition is absolutely true or if a value is absolute, still we are never in a position to *verify* that a particular value or religious doctrine is absolute. The *concept* of the absolute remains meaningful and important in human thought, nonetheless, because it ever reminds us that there *may* be something better (truer or more valuable) than that to which we are presently committed.

To be sure, we can and should commit ourselves absolutely to that which is absolutely good and absolutely true, but such a commitment is a commitment to form, not to content. It is a *disposition* to commit ourselves absolutely when we discover that which is absolute. But it tells us nothing about which *specific* things are absolute. Moreover, to commit ourselves absolutely to the good and the true would entail never committing ourselves absolutely to anything specific and concrete. Why? Because since we do not have the wherewithal to know whether some specific thing is absolute, to commit ourselves to it absolutely would be to risk forever excluding ourselves from that which is better and, ultimately, from that which is best. Hence, rigid commitment is potentially self-defeating, or at least it is so if we desire to be committed to that which *is* best and not simply to that which *seems* best at the moment. Distressing, of course, is the fact that even if we do somehow fix upon that which is perfectly good or true in religion, we will not be able to justify our conviction that it is such. Further, as Bertrand Russell points out in *Mysticism and Logic,* the very intensity of emotion involved in mystical intuition is one of its drawbacks, for it tends to lead us to assume that we *know* what we only believe or *feel.* Indeed, some people may find so frustrating the contention that we cannot know the absolute that they may block out the distinction between feeling that something is the truth and knowing that it is the truth. I can sympathize with them, but I cannot agree with them.

Yet, is the idea of the absolute simply an infuriating tease, since we could stare the absolute in the face without being able to justify our belief (conviction, feeling, intuition) that it is the absolute? This frustration, it seems to me, is an inescapable aspect of the human situation. I can commit myself *absolutely* to that which creates and sustains human good, but I can commit myself only *tentatively* to those specific things that create and sustain human good.[2] Why only tentatively? Because I must keep myself open to the possible appearance of something better. We must, then, combine *both commitment and openness.* It is in *refusal to admit* that there may be something better that we become idolatrous by absolutizing a particular, and it is idolatry which leads to close-mindedness, dogmatism, and exclusiveness. It is in *refusal to commit* ourselves that we perish—or, more likely, that we blind ourselves to that to which we are in fact committed. Moreover, openness without commitment is pointless (since the point of being open is to discover and enjoy something good or better), and commitment without openness is self-contradictory (since we want to be committed to the best that there *is* and we can never know whether we already are). Hence, we should live according to the best that we know and keep ourselves open to the better—which is not as easy as it may sound, given the temptations and distractions, the habits and fears, the prejudices and ignorance that afflict us.

I can imagine someone, a Buddhist, let's say, responding at this point, "But I have compared Buddha to Moses and Jesus and Krishna, and he *is* the best!" This is a legitimate and important kind of response, but it needs to be understood within the following context of analysis. First, given a finite set of objects, $x$, $y$, and $z$, it is legitimate for a person to make the personal judgment, "$x$ is the best," meaning, "In my opinion, $x$ is better than $y$ or $z$." With an *infinite* set of objects, however—and this is my second point—the best that a person can say is still some form of "$x$ is better than $y$ or $z$." To claim to know that $x$ is the best of an *infinite* set is always illegitimate because we can never examine all the members of an infinite set. Hence, we can compare $x$ only to those members of the set we *have* examined. We can even endeavor to compare $x$ to every extant religion, but given the number of existing religions, atheistic as well as theistic, and given the fact that the smallest among them must be taken as seriously as the largest (the largest at present—if it is still Christianity and not communism—began as a baker's dozen), this hardly seems like a task which could be completed in one lifetime. And even if by sheer dint of energy you did complete it and still judged $x$ best, it would always be possible that a new religion would eventually appear which you yourself would judge to be better than $x$. Hence, if the set of possible objects of religious commitment is infinite, as it seems to be, then while it is perfectly legitimate for a person to say of the object of his religious devotion, "It is *unsurpassed* in my life," it would be illegitimate for him to say, "It is *unsurpassable.*" The former he may know; the latter he cannot. Further, the fact that a person cannot at the moment *imagine* anything eclipsing the object of his present religious devotion is not to be taken as evidence that his object of devotion cannot be surpassed. Rather, his inability in this respect is to be expected, for religious devotion in its purest sense is precisely devotion to that than which we neither know nor can imagine anything greater. But knowledge and imagination both, of course, can be expanded in ways and to an extent that one would have hitherto not believed possible. Indeed, that kind of radical expansion of "mind, heart, and soul" is what is involved in religious conversion.

Now let's return to the question raised in the opening paragraph of this chapter: If we do not know what is absolute, then we cannot judge varying degrees of approximation to the absolute; so how can we judge with confidence whether one thing is really better than another? First, we must recognize that the individual is always the final judge as to whether something is religiously better than something else. The only judgments about religious worth that are relevant to human beings are those made by human beings, for human beings are the criteria as well as the judges of the worth of religious ideas and practices. This does not mean that the individual's judgments about religious matters are always correct. It means only that in the final analysis, it is the individual who must judge the worth of a religious doctrine or practice, and he can judge it only out of his own experience. The standard of religious worth does not lie outside us like a yardstick. To repeat, we as individuals are the criteria and the judges of religious worth, for what religion is largely about is the achievement of self-knowledge and self-realization—whether within a theistic, a naturalistic, or some other metaphysical framework. We cannot assay that $x$ is better than $y$ by comparing them both to the absolute and seeing which is closer, but we can assay which is better in terms of our own life experience. And if we cannot have confidence in ourselves, then we can have confidence in nothing—since if we decide to place our trust in something other than ourselves, it is the self that must decide what it is that is more worthy of confidence than itself. Hence, confidence in oneself must precede confidence in anything else. This does not mean that the self can think of reality however it likes. Reality is what it is; our *understanding* of reality is composed of those ideas which—for whatever reasons—are most convincing to us. Ideally, I suggest, we should compose our understanding of reality out of those ideas which help us live our lives in the most successful and encouraging manner. Here you might reflect back on my claim that a healthy religious faith is optimistic and that religious faith plays an aesthetic role in human life. It is aesthetic not in the sense that it is fictitious, but in the sense that it enhances the significance and the beauty of one's life.

To summarize, mature religious commitment involves (1) commitment to the best that we know now, (2) recognition that we cannot prove that there is nothing better, (3) and openness to the possible appearance of something better. The proper focus of *absolute* commitment, however, is not to anything specific—even though it be humanity, love, or Jesus. Rather, it should be to that kind of openness which makes us susceptible to something better than we have now—if it exists and when it appears to us. Absolute commitment of this kind is not dogmatic, for it is not a matter of absolute commitment to anything specific; hence, every specific commitment remains open to fundamental examination. Nor does this kind of absolute commitment lead necessarily to romanticism—that is, to following one's fancy of the moment, no matter how quickly it might change. Why not romanticism? Because *absolute commitment* to the really good and true should be accompanied by *disciplined defeasible commitment* to the high points of our lives. This second kind of commitment gives us a kind of depth against which superficiality cannot prevail, but without giving us the illusion that the object of our commitment is unsurpassable. We do not have an absolute criterion regarding matters religious, so we have no right to claim that one thing is absolutely better than another.

We do sometimes have the *personal* experience of one thing being *better* than another, and it is by such personal experiences of "better" that we can find authority and direction for our lives. We must learn to cultivate our sensitivity and loyalty to such experiences without assuming that they must be regarded as absolute. Indeed, it seems to me that our situation is very much like that of Hesiod's "flying spiders." Miguel de Unamuno reports on this phenomenon in *The Agony of Christianity:*

> The name of "Threads of the Virgin" is applied to certain tiny threads that float in the wind and on which a certain kind of spiders—which Hesiod . . . calls flying spiders—take flight in the free breezes of the air and even in the midst of a violent storm. There are also such things as winged seeds, equipped with tufts. But these spiders spin those floating threads out of their own entrails, delicate webs by means of which they hurl themselves into space unknown. What an awesome symbol of faith![3]

And so it is, for we too must spin a web of religion from the entrails of our own experience and hurl ourselves upon it into space and time unknown— hoping that the web will sustain us through the storms and will dance in the breezes—rarely aware of how delicate a thing it really is.

**Footnotes**

1. Frederick Streng, *Understanding Religious Man* (Belmont, Calif.: Dickenson Publishing Co., Inc., 1969), p. 126.

2. I first encountered the idea of dual commitment (absolute and tentative) in a lecture by Henry Nelson Wieman. He elaborates this idea in his *Man's Ultimate Commitment* (Carbondale, Ill.: Southern Illinois University Press, 1958), pp. 21, 167–169.

3. Miguel de Unamuno, *The Agony of Christianity* (New York: Frederick Ungar Publishing Co., 1960), pp. 76–77.

# The Spiral
# of Religious Growth

QUESTIONS TO THINK ABOUT

- What are four phases of the cycle of religious growth? Name and describe each.
- What are some of Rudolf Otto's main points about the nature of religious experience?
- What are some of Martin Buber's main points about the nature of religious faith?
- What are some of Carl Jung's main points about religion?
- What are some of Abraham Maslow's main points about religious experience?
- What distinction does Philip Phenix make between "the life of desire" and "the life of loyalty"?
- What does Abraham Heschel mean when he says that "*faith is faithfulness,* loyalty to an event, loyalty to our response"?
- What is the difference between the "way of Greece" and "the way of Israel"?

- What is worship? What is its function and structure in human life?
- Do people do only what they enjoy?
- Should we worship only when we feel like it?
- Should we worship together or alone?
- Why is religious growth a spiral and not just a cycle?
- What causes the cycle of religious growth to begin again?

So far, I have been doing a kind of structural analysis of religious commitment, looking from a static point of view at the way it's built and the parts that make it up. Now I would like to do a process analysis—that is, take a look at religious involvement as something that is moving, growing, developing. I see this process as cyclical in nature and passing through four fundamental phases. These phases can be described as follows: (1) the stage of pursuit, (2) the moment of revelation, (3) the moment of response, and (4) the stage of action. Most adults have been through this cycle many times—though they may not have noticed its structure or how the successive phases contributed to their personal growth. To be human and to escape this cycle altogether seems most unlikely. Let's take a look at each of the four phases.

## THE STAGE OF PURSUIT

The first stage of the religious cycle, the launching pad, so to speak, is the stage of pursuit—the stage of the restless heart, of intense yearning that the void within might be filled, of profound anxiety at the prospect of ultimate meaninglessness. Something of the spirit of this moment is reflected in Psalm 42 in which the psalmist writes, "As a hart longs for flowing streams, so longs my soul for thee, O God. My soul thirsts for God, for the living God." Also, "Why are you cast down, O my soul, and why are you disquieted within me?"[1] Clearly, the present beliefs, practices, and experiences of such a person are felt as inadequate. Something *more* is desired—but what? Perhaps the most fundamental truth about religion is that it is the endeavor to provide that "something more" which brings a sense of closure to the meaning of our lives. Different religions bring about that sense in radically different ways, ranging from the very specific proposals of theistic religions (recall Augustine's statement: "Our hearts are restless 'till they find their rest in Thee") to the Zen Buddhist claim that our yearning is not an emptiness to be filled by reason or revelation, but a sickness to be cured. But all religions, as far as I can tell, major in helping us cope with our personal metaphysical uneasiness.[2]

## THE MOMENT OF REVELATION

The moment of revelation is the moment at which there comes an answer to our question, a reply to our plea, a response to our groping, something that comes from we know not where and invades our consciousness. This is a necessary moment if religious concern is ever to pass over into religious faith, for the religious struggle is precisely with problems we feel unable to resolve by ourselves. As Carl Jung states, "Man is never helped in his suffering by what he thinks for himself, but only by revelations of wisdom greater than his own. It is this which lifts him out of his distress."[3] Such a revelation may be from a natural or a supernatural source; we are not concerned with that question here. But if the moment of revelation had never come at all—whatever its origin—religious faith would have never been born, for how can a person become religious if something of great value, indeed, of seeming ultimate value, has not impressed itself upon him?

Yet, what is it that is revealed to us? What is the nature of revelation? What is the cause of religious experience? These are questions that have been answered in conflicting ways, even by persons who all value religious experience highly. Consequently, what I would like to do now is to share with you some of the range of opinion of persons who all believe in the value of religious experience: Rudolf Otto, author of classic works in phenomenology of religion and mysticism; Martin Buber, Jewish existentialist philosopher, best known for his distinctions between I, Thou, and It; Carl Jung, founder of the analytic school of psychology, which emphasizes archetypes and the collective unconscious; and Abraham Maslow, who tried to make psychology more accessible and relevant to every person.

### *Rudolf Otto*

I would like to introduce you to Rudolf Otto's analysis of religious experience. Otto was a German philosopher/theologian who lived from 1869 to 1937 and made many important contributions to the study of religious experience. He was a profound student of the world's religions and an energetic world traveler. Hence, his book, *Mysticism: East and West,* was not just a product of library research. His sensitivity and openness to all religions was a result of his belief that all religions are the result of different people's interactions with one divine reality. A long-standing dream came true when he succeeded in establishing in Germany an institute for the comparative study of the living faiths of the world. Otto's best known book, *The Idea of the Holy,* was published in 1923 and is still considered by many the finest analysis of religious experience ever written. It is to some of the main ideas of that book that we turn our attention now.

*First,* Otto claims that religious experience is a *distinctive* kind of experience which is not to be understood as some other kind of experience in disguise—such as an especially intense aesthetic experience, or a feeling of oneness with Nature, or an uplifting experience resulting from participation in a social cause.[4] *Second,* Otto claims that there is *no* religion in which religious experience does not live as its "real innermost core." Hence, religious experience is the life blood of religion, and a religion devoid of religious experience is no longer truly a religion, any more than a corpse is truly a person. *Third,* we can talk about religious experience, but we must do so obliquely and by means of metaphors. Why? Because our language is based on the categories of natural experience—categories such as color, shape, size, and location—but religious experience is not comparable to natural experience. The categories of natural sensory experience simply do not apply literally to the nature and content of religious experience. Hence, we should not expect our language to do a clear job of describing religious experience. Still, it's all we've got, so we must do with it the best that we can, realizing its limitations. *Fourth,* Otto claims that the religious experience is *of* something, or at least so it feels. It is an experience in which we feel that we are up against something, that something has encountered us. It is not as though we were daydreaming or imagining. Otto gives the name "numen" to this special something which we feel ourselves to be up against and he attributes to it the following five characteristics: (1) absolute unapproachability, (2) absolute overpoweringness, (3) energy or urgency, (4) wholly other, (5) fascinating, intoxicating. Let's take a closer look at each of these traits.

*First,* the numen has the characteristic of absolute unapproachability. It provokes within us a kind of dread, a *religious dread.* Otto insists that this kind of dread is not like *natural fear,* of a snake, say; nor is it like *anxiety,* for example, that your plane will be hijacked. It is another kind of thing altogether. "It first begins to stir," Otto writes, "in the feeling of 'something *uncanny,'* *'eerie,'* or *'weird.'* " This is an experience that tears us from our ordinary state of mind, shudders through us with an alarmingly disorienting effect, and leaves us convinced that there are dangerous powers and forces of which we are not aware in our everyday mode of consciousness. Otto goes on to say that "it is this feeling which, emerging in the mind of primeval man, forms the starting-point for the entire religious development in history."[5] This awe of the numen can cause a shudder which is well-depicted in Isaiah's experience, recorded in Chapter 6 of the book of Isaiah in the Bible. The language there is highly symbolic, but the character of Isaiah's emotion is conveyed quite effectively:

> In the year that King Uzziah died I saw the Lord sitting upon a throne, high and lifted up; and his train filled the temple. Above him stood the seraphim; each had six wings: with two he covered his face, and with two he covered his

feet, and with two he flew. And one called to another and said: "Holy, holy, holy is the Lord of hosts; the whole earth is full of his glory." And the foundations of the thresholds shook at the voice of him who called, and the house was filled with smoke. And I said: "Woe is me! For I am lost; for I am a man of unclean lips; for my eyes have seen the King, the Lord of hosts!"

The *second* characteristic encountered in the numen is might, power, indeed, "absolute overpoweringness." Again we can think of earthly examples of being overpowered, such as in a very uneven wrestling match, but the analogy must fail ultimately, for in our earthly experience we find that we are at least able to exert ourselves—no matter how ineffectively— against that which overpowers us. But in the religious experience we are pervaded with the feeling that we have been confronted by absolute power, to which we can offer no resistance whatsoever. "Thus," Otto writes, "in contrast to 'the overpowering' of which we are conscious as an object over against the self, there is the feeling of one's own submergence, of being but 'dust and ashes' and nothingness. And this forms the numinous raw material for the feeling of religious humility."[6] It gives rise also to a feeling of the "awful majesty" of the divine.

*Third,* the object of religious experience is characterized by "urgency" or "energy." As the Bible puts it, the Lord God is a living God, an active, passionate, vital, forceful God who neither sleeps nor rests. Naturalists talk about Nature, rather than God, as a pulsating, dynamic, flowing process whose vitality we can apprehend in mystic moments. This element of religious experience has given rise to quarrels between the mystics and some philosophers, such as Aristotle, who describe the divine in terms of static concepts. God for these philosophers is without motion, without passion, and without volition, whereas the mystics claim that their experiences of the divine reveal something "urgent, active, compelling, and alive."[7] Logical consideration drove some philosophers to conclude that a perfect being could not have passions (since they would destroy its perfect state of bliss), and would not will anything, since it lacks nothing. But the mystics were unwilling to deny their sense that it was a perfect being which had entered their lives and established a relationship with them.

Otto writes, "We gave to the object to which the numinous consciousness is directed the name *'mysterium tremendum.'* "[8] In his exposition of the meaning of this phrase he explains the *tremendum* aspect of the numinous object in terms of the three elements we have already explored: *awefulness, majesty,* and *energy.* The *mysterium* aspect of the numinous he explains in terms of the other two elements of the religious experience: its "wholly otherness" and its aura of fascination. Let's take a brief look at these last two elements.

*Fourth,* Otto is quick to point out that the "mysteriousness" of the numinosum is not like the "ordinary" mysteries of life—the latter being things that puzzle us but that are capable of explanation. Rather, what we are up against in religious experience is something wholly other than anything we have ever experienced in the realms of nature and society. It is "that which is quite beyond the sphere of the usual, the intelligible, and the familiar, which therefore falls quite outside the limits of the 'canny,' and is contrasted with it, filling the mind with blank wonder and astonishment."[9]

But the profundity of the mystery of the numinosum goes even deeper than this, for the feeling we get is that it is "*beyond* our apprehension and comprehension, not only because our knowledge has certain irremovable limits, but because in it we come upon something inherently 'wholly other,' whose kind and character are incommensurable with our own, and before which we therefore recoil in a wonder that strikes us chill and numb."[10] Mystics in all ages and all cultures have been aware of this wholly-other quality of the object of religious experience. Consequently, they have combined philosophy and humor to say that the numinosum is "nothing." What is God? Nothing. What are you praying to, meditating upon, seeking unity with? Nothing. There is a kind of honesty in this answer which there can be in no other because that which is being prayed to or contemplated or merged with cannot be referred to literally by any word or combination of words in any language. It isn't anything we can describe or point to—so we say, with a bit of a smile, "It is nothing." At the same time, however, mysticism affirms "the *positive quality* of the 'wholly other' as a very living factor in its overbrimming religious emotion."[11] The numinosum is not just an idea. Nor is it like an unsighted planet whose existence is known only through intellectual calculations. Rather, it has a direct and deeply felt personal impact. "It is through this positive feeling-content that the concepts of the 'transcendent' and 'supernatural' become forthwith designations for a unique 'wholly other' reality and quality, something of whose special character we can *feel*, without being able to give it clear conceptual expression."[12] To illustrate this, let me tell a story about a Hindu father who was asked by his child, "What is God?" The father's now famous response was, "Neti, neti," meaning, "Neither this nor that." That is, the father pointed to something, perhaps a chair, and said, "God is not that." Then he pointed to something else, perhaps a dog, and said, "That is not God." On and on he went from one thing to another, saying "neither this nor that is God," until finally the child got the point: God cannot be identified with any thing in this world or with the world itself. Hence, in terms of the things of this world, revealed to us by our senses, God is nothing; and yet, the fact that God is nothing in terms of the things of this world does not mean that God is nothing at all. Indeed, that He is wholly other than anything in this world and yet is something very real is precisely part of the conviction which one carries away from religious experience.[13]

The *fifth* and final element which Otto analyzes out of the religious experience is that of *fascination*. The mystery of the numen is not simply

something to be wondered at; it is something that entrances us, that capti-
vates and transports us "with a strange ravishment, rising often enough to
the pitch of dizzy intoxication."[14] Otto acknowledges that there are
similarities between this aspect of religious experience and certain aspects of
ordinary experience. Love, mercy, pity, comfort, are all experienced in
ordinary life and can also be present in religious experience, though in the
latter they are experienced in their perfection. Likewise, experiencing the
wrath or rage of God is not totally unlike the small child's experience of the
wrath of a parent. Still, the content of religious experience, according to
those who have undergone it, can in no way be reduced to these natural
experiences taken to a higher level of intensity.

> Bliss or beatitude is more, far more, than the mere natural feeling of being
> comforted, of reliance, of the joy of love, however these may be heightened
> and enhanced. Just as "wrath," taken in a purely rational or a purely ethical
> sense, does not exhaust that profound element of *awefulness* which is locked
> in the mystery of deity, so neither does "graciousness" exhaust the profound
> element of *wonderfulness* and rapture which lies in the mysterious beatific
> experience of deity.[15]

By virtue of its fascinating quality, the numinous becomes the object
of personal search, desire, and yearning. In fact, once the numen has been
experienced, "possession of and by the numen becomes an end in itself; it
begins to be sought for its own sake; and the wildest and most artificial
methods of asceticism are put into practice to attain it." Otto continues,

> Here, too, commences the process of development by which the experience is
> matured and purified, till finally it reaches its consummation in the sublimest
> and purest states of the "life within the Spirit" and in the noblest mysticism.
> Widely various as these states are in themselves, yet they have this element in
> common, that in them the mysterium is experienced in its essential, positive,
> and specific character, as something that bestows upon man a beatitude
> beyond compare . . . one whose real nature he can neither proclaim in speech
> nor conceive in thought, but may know only by a direct and living experience.[16]

Otto goes on to claim that in religious experience is revealed

> an *ideal good* known only to religion and in its nature fundamentally non-
> rational [that is, unable to be apprehended in terms of the categories of nature],
> which the mind knows of in yearning and presentiment, recognizing it for what
> it is behind the obscure and inadequate symbols which are its only expression.
> And this shows that above and beyond our rational [self] lies hidden *the
> ultimate and highest part of our nature,* which can find no satisfaction in the
> mere allaying of the needs of our sensuous, psychical, or intellectual impulses
> and cravings.[17]

If you've paid close attention, you realize now that we have gone from
the negative to the positive pole of religious experience. Otto started out

with the element of *religious dread* and he has ended up with the element of *religious fascination*. It is precisely the contrast of these two elements that provides the *profound tension* of religious experience—at once a feeling of dread and of rapture, of repulsion and attraction. These two contrary feelings combine in "a strange harmony of contrasts" to which mystics across the centuries have testified. Interestingly enough, if theists are correct that the *cause* of religious experience is a supreme personal being, then we *should expect* the religious experience to be "a strange harmony of contrasts"—since it would be, at one and the same time, an experience of a reality which is infinitely more powerful and frightening than any natural force and infinitely more fascinating than its most captivating creation.

### Martin Buber

Buber, a Jewish philosopher/theologian of the twentieth century, spent much of his life elucidating what he called "the I–Thou relationship" and distinguishing it from the I–It relationship. Buber was convinced that for human beings there are two basic modes of relating to something. You can relate to it as an It—that is, as a thing, a passive object—or you can relate to it in a manner of mutuality, as a Thou. Buber illustrates the difference between the two types of relationship (and also illustrates that we can relate to the same object as an It or as a Thou) by asking us to consider "the child that silently speaks to his mother through nothing other than looking into her eyes and the child that looks at something on the mother as at any other object. . . ."[18] To make the illustration a bit more pointed, consider the difference between the child looking at the mother's eyes to see what color they are and the child looking into the mother's eyes in wonder and affection. In the former act the eyes may be no more than an object of curiosity; in the latter act they are a passageway through which something is expressed and from which a response is sought.

The question with which we are primarily concerned is whether a conscious relation with God is an I–It relationship or an I–Thou relationship. Blaise Pascal, a seventeenth-century, many-sided genius, pointed out that for many philosophers, God is a concept, an It, not a person, a Thou.[19] A good twentieth-century example of such a philosopher is John Dewey. In his book, *A Common Faith,* Dewey states that to him the word "God" means "the unity of all ideal ends arousing us to desire and actions."[20] That is, for Dewey the word "God" refers to that idealized vision of the world which is so attractive that it causes us to act in order to actualize it. Clearly, such a God is an idea and not a person. Another impersonal conception of God was set forth in the nineteenth century by Ludwig Feuerbach. The word "God," according to Feuerbach, refers to an idealized conception of Man. This ideal conception is built up in our imagination by means of projecting onto an imaginary person whatever virtues and powers we believe would constitute human perfection. This process occurs unwittingly, of course. The believer does not realize the source of his idea of God. Rather, he operates under the illusion that he is relating to a divine person, only he isn't. Once one becomes aware of the origin of the God idea, one need not reject the God idea itself, since it represents one's highest conception of man, but one can no longer presume to relate to God as to a person.

These explanations by Dewey and by Feuerbach are explanations of what is happening in religious experience. In the one case, we are being aroused by a utopian vision; in the other, we are being ennobled by an image of the powers and capacities of Man. But we must ask whether these explanations are any more adequate than theistic explanations which explain religious experience in terms of the presence of a divine person. Can all cases of religious experience be accounted for in terms of the impersonalistic explanations of Dewey and Feuerbach? Experiences called "religious" are quite diverse, of course, but impersonalistic explanations, Buber argues, cannot account satisfactorily for religious experiences that are paradigmatic in the biblical tradition—namely, those religious experiences in which we feel ourselves to be up against a very real though non-sensory person. We don't account for I–Thou encounters with another human being in terms of purely impersonalistic explanations—though we could. Much less, then, should we account for a *religious* I–Thou experience in impersonalistic terms, since the I–Thou experience finds its purest, most powerful expression precisely in religious experience. In Buber's own words, "I–Thou finds its highest intensity and transfiguration in religious reality, in which unlimited Being becomes, as absolute person, my partner."[21]

The Thou of religious experience is, according to Buber, the living God who approaches us and addresses us as individuals in our own concrete circumstances. Hence, religious experience in the biblical sense is an encounter in which we are convinced that we are over against someone who is real and living, and not simply a concept which is a synthesis of ideals. You might well be thinking, "But how do you know a divine person is really there and that you are not deluded?" Buber would agree that there is no way to *prove* that you are not deceived—but that is true with regard to *every* experience! How can you *prove* you are not dreaming now? Perhaps Pascal is right that "life is a dream a little less inconstant"?[22] When you talk to a person, how can you *prove* that behind that person's skin there is listening, caring, feeling, imagining? Isn't it true that when you talk to a person you do not mean to be talking to his body and nothing more? When you look lovingly into someone's eyes and tell her your appreciation for something she has done, isn't it true that you are not looking *at* her eyes and speaking *to* her ears but are communicating to what, somehow, lies "at the end" of those sense organs? And the fact that you have never "seen" that person's "mind," so as to be sure that she isn't a mindless, emotionless robot, doesn't stop you from entering into an I–Thou relationship with her. You trust your intuition that you are in the presence of a human person, and not merely of a human body; so why not trust your intuition, when it occurs, that you are in the presence of a divine person?[23]

To trust your feeling that you *have* encountered the living God does not, according to Buber, mean that you should be able to *speak* about God. Recall for a moment the limitations of ordinary language which we noted in the section on Otto. Buber claims that our lack of a language with which to describe God literally is no problem at all. "It is not necessary to know something about God," he writes, "in order really to believe in Him: many true believers know how to talk *to* God but not *about* Him. If one dares to turn toward the unknown God, to go to meet Him, to call to Him, Reality is present."[24] To be sure, there is a kind of knowledge acquired from encounter with God, but it is not the kind of knowledge that can be externalized for public investigation or that can be set forth in the categories of ordinary language. Public knowledge is the kind we acquire from I–It relationships. God we never encounter as an It. Hence, those people are mistaken who believe that the knowledge acquired from religious experience should be externalizable and open to public inquiry. To quote Buber's difficult but exquisite language, "Philosophy errs in . . . regarding the essence of religion as the knowledge of an object which is indifferent to being known."[25] Buber has in mind here such philosophers as Aristotle and Epicurus, ancient Greeks who believed that God is real but, in His perfect state of bliss, oblivious to the affairs of earth and the attentions of human beings. Indeed, Epicurus argued, should God choose to become involved with the human species, He would quickly lose His perfect peace of mind—and for the thanks He would get, we can be sure He won't do that! This conception of God contrasts sharply, of course, with the biblical conception that Buber affirms. The Living God, the God of Abraham, Isaac, and Jacob, is never indifferent to the attentions of human beings. And insofar as the Bible speaks of "knowledge of God," it does not portray it as the abstract, intellectual relation

> of a thinking subject to a neutral object of thought, but rather as *mutual contact,* as the *genuinely reciprocal meeting* in the fullness of life between one active existence and another. Similarly, religion understands *faith* as the entrance into this reciprocity, as binding oneself in relationship with an undemonstrable and unprovable, yet even so, in relationship, knowable Being, from whom all meaning comes.[26]

Clearly, Buber is using the word "know" in a different sense than we used in Chapter 6. He is using it in the sense in which we say that we "know" or are "getting to know" a person. Entry into such a relationship of give and take requires faith that the other is really a person, a subject with depth, as well as an object with surfaces. God and God alone is *pure* subject, presenting no aspects that can be studied without His awareness and regard.

Because the living God is absolute subject and never mere object, the Second Commandment warns against making images of God. An image or a symbol is an "it," something impersonal, and it will likely seduce us into relating primarily to it rather than to God, the symbol thereby becoming an idol. To be sure, idols are much more comfortable to relate to than the divine person, who stands over us in judgment as well as by us in love, but idols eventually prove disillusioning or tragic. The only appropriate relationship, indeed, the only *possible* relationship to the Absolute is a direct I–Thou relationship, for the Absolute is in no way nor at any time indifferent to our approach. I may be unaware that someone is paying attention to me. God is never unaware of attention paid to Him. I may not *care* that someone is paying attention to me. God, according to Buber, always cares.

You might ask at this point, "But what about the notorious silence of God in the hearts of modern persons?" Indeed, isn't Jean-Paul Sartre's rejection of God based in part on the silence of God? The answer here is "yes." Sartre, the most famous atheist existentialist of our century, reportedly once stepped from a train and announced to the waiting press corps, "Gentlemen, God is dead!" It is absurd, Sartre argues, for people to persevere in their theism in the face of divine silence. "God is dead!" That is, there never was a real God, and now even the *idea* of God is defunct! We must acknowledge this, gird ourselves with courage, and follow out the consequences of living in a Godless universe.[27]

Buber, to the contrary, sees no reason to conclude that God's silence implies God's death. The biblical tradition reports periods of divine silence at least as far back as the time of Isaiah (sixth century B.C.), and most Judeo-Christian thinkers have had something to say about God's *hiddenness* as well as His *presence*. To illustrate his point, Buber points out that *an eclipse is something which takes place between the sun and our eyes.*[28] It is not something which takes place *in* the sun; it does not mean that the sun is dead. Likewise, with regard to the silence of God, "It would be worthier," Buber writes, perhaps with Sartre in mind, "not to explain it to oneself in sensational and incompetent sayings, such as that of the 'death' of God, but to endure it as it is and at the same time to move existentially toward a new happening, toward that event in which the word between heaven and earth will again be heard."[29] Meanwhile, the perseverance of the religious need in people's lives does not reveal in these people an insecure refusal to face the truth, as Sartre claims it does. Nor does such a longing contradict the meaning of the silence of God. Rather, it reveals the confidence and trust of those who have known God and are willing to wait for the return of His felt presence. And while we are waiting in patient trust, Buber proposes, we should reflect upon the impact and meaning of God's silence and ask, "Why?"

A final word from Buber. He claims that genuine encounter with the Eternal Thou confirms the biblical teaching that all religious life begins with "the fear of God." It begins, he writes, "when our existence between birth and death becomes incomprehensible and uncanny, when all security is shattered through the mystery."[30] Then he issues this warning:

> He who begins with the love of God without having previously experienced the fear of God, loves an idol which he himself has made, a god whom it is easy enough to love. He does not love the real God who is, to begin with, dreadful and incomprehensible. Consequently, if he then perceives . . . that God is dreadful and incomprehensible, he is terrified. He despairs of God and the world if God does not take pity on him . . . and bring him to love Him Himself.[31]

Presumably this means something like what Alfred North Whitehead meant in *Religion in the Making* (see footnotes for Chapter 4) when he said that religious maturation consists in moving from "God the void" (when God is a matter of indifference to us), to "God the enemy" (when God is a source of torment to us), to "God the companion" (when God is a blessing to us). Interestingly, perhaps significantly, all three persons, Otto, Buber, and Whitehead, claim that when religious consciousness follows its full course, it begins in a negative mode but ends in a positive one.

### Carl Jung

Whereas Otto and Buber are theists in a traditional sense, our next object of study, Carl Jung, is not. Yet neither is he an atheist. He falls somewhere between these two extremes in spite of the fact that he was a long-time student and associate of Sigmund Freud, one of the twentieth century's most trenchant critics of religion. Jung developed a profound sensitivity to and appreciation for religion and its importance in human life. In fact, after thirty-two years of research and practice as a psychiatrist, he made the statement we mentioned in Chapter 2:

> Among all my patients in the second half of life—that is to say over thirty-five—there has not been one whose problem in the last resort was not that of finding a religious outlook on life. It is safe to say that every one of them fell ill because he had lost that which the living religions of every age have given to their followers, and none of them has been really healed who did not regain his religious outlook.[32]

Jung is quick to add that regaining a religious outlook does not depend on adopting some particular creed or joining a particular religious organization. Nor does he mean that one must gain back the same religious outlook one had as a child. What he does mean is very complicated. It is founded on his conception of the unconscious, and we cannot take the time to examine that concept here.[33] I would like, however, to focus briefly on some of his insights into the second phase of the religious cycle—i.e., religious experience. These ideas can all be found in his *Psychology and Religion*.

In that book Jung writes that by the word "religion" he means "a careful and scrupulous observation" of that which Rudolf Otto meant by the word "numinosum." More fully, religion is

a careful consideration and observation of certain dynamic factors, understood to be "powers," spirits, demons, gods, laws, he had found in his world powerful, dangerous or helpful enough to be taken into careful consideration, or grand, beautiful and meaningful enough to be devoutly adored and loved.[34]

Briefly, religion in its positive mode is the zealous cultivation and enjoyment of that which is most precious to us. In its negative mode it consists of the fearful attention and concessions paid to that by which we are most alarmed.

In either case, negative or positive, it is important to notice that the numinosum is something which happens *to* us. It comes to us. It is not and cannot be caused by an act of will on our part. Rather,

it seizes and controls the human subject, which is always rather its victim than its creator. The numinosum is an involuntary condition of the subject, whatever its cause may be. At all events, religious teaching as well as [the opinions of people] always and everywhere explains this condition as being due to a cause external to the individual. The numinosum is either a quality of a visible object or the influence of an invisible presence causing a peculiar alteration of consciousness.[35]

In fact, Jung adds, the word "religion" might be used to designate "the attitude peculiar to a consciousness which has been altered by the experience of the numinosum."[36] Such an experience in its positive mode elicits from us loyalty, trust, confidence, and devotion to that which we believe to have brought about our new state of mind.

Jung is quick to point out that there is a profound difference between *religious sentimentality* and the *numinosum of religious experience.* The latter is a powerful, transforming force that lifts us out of the world only to plunge us back into it, giving us new direction, new strength, new joy, and a set of marching orders. The former, by contrast, is a melancholy state of mind; it is wistful pleasure found in childhood reminiscences; it is a mild but passive yearning for a better state of world affairs. Moreover, sentimentality is "the well-known characteristic of a religion that has lost the living mystery."[37] I would add that it is tragic when an outsider (or an insider!) mistakes sentimentality for the root of religion—since then he will never understand the great religions that have rocked the world and of which the sentimental religions are only faded variations. It is tragic also when someone who has lost contact with the numinous rests content thenceforth with religious sentimentality, for such a religion will be a weak and lukewarm cup of tea when what is needed is hot and nourishing broth.

If we turn our attention now to the *value* of religious experience, we find Jung once again in agreement with Rudolf Otto, who, you will recall, talks about the unique value of religious experience. Jung claims that to those who have it, religious experience is not just one more valuable kind of experience. Rather, "if it means anything, it means everything to those who have it." And surely if we want to know the value of religious experience, we should ask what it means to those who have had it rather than consulting the skeptics. Jung goes on to say, in character with our earlier analysis, "One could even define religious experience as that kind of experience which is characterized by the highest appreciation, no matter what its contents are."[38]

Later he states that religion itself is one's relationship to the highest or strongest value in one's experience, whether that value be a positive one or a negative one, whether it enchants or frightens. Then he makes a point that goes right to the heart of the second phase of the religious cycle. Still speaking about religion as one's relationship to the highest or strongest value in one's experience, he points out that the relationship can be "voluntary as well as involuntary." The "as well as" indicates that the relationship is involuntary to start with, and so it is, for our deity is always that psychological factor by which we are overwhelmed. However, we can be innocently unaware of what it is, or we can try to convince ourselves and others that it isn't what it is, or we can acknowledge what it is and self-consciously affirm it. In Jung's words, "you can accept, consciously, the value by which you are possessed unconsciously." You can allow it to surface fully in your consciousness, or, if you will, to reveal itself.

Jung goes on to say that whenever a god "ceases to be an overwhelming factor, he becomes a mere name. His essence is dead and his power is gone."[39] Any further devotion to such a god must be a matter of self-delusion, hypocrisy, sentimentality, or mindless routine. But surely you should not accept religious sentimentality in place of numinous experience, and you should not force yourself to remain committed to a god that no longer empowers you.[40]

Jung concludes *Psychology and Religion* by defending from skeptics the legitimacy and importance of religious experience. He writes:

> Religious experience is absolute. It is indisputable. You can only say that you have never had such an experience, and your opponent will say: "Sorry, I have." And there your discussion will come to an end. No matter what the world thinks about religious experience, the one who has it possesses the great treasure of a thing that has provided him with a source of life, meaning and beauty and that has given a new splendor to the world and to mankind. He has pistis [faith] and peace. Where is the criterium by which you could say that such a life is not legitimate, that such experience is not valid and that such pistis is mere illusion? Is there, as a matter of fact, any better truth about ultimate things than the one that helps you to live? Nobody can know what the ultimate things are. We must, therefore, take them as we experience them. And if such experience helps to make your life healthier, more beautiful, more

complete and more satisfactory to yourself and to those you love, you may safely say: "This was the grace of God."[41]

These, then, are some of Carl Jung's ideas on religion, and I would like to emphasize two of them, in closing. First, religion is not man-made—at least not in the sense that chairs and maps are. A religion is not something that can be created on the drawing board, so to say. It is not the product of the conscious ego. At the very least it is the product of the unconscious ego—and it may be much more. It wells up from deep within us—we know not whence or how. Hence, Jung's position is an implicit criticism of those people who want to construct a "rational religion" founded on human reason. Such a religion would be at best like boiled water—clear but flat. The second point is that religious experience is not merely an intensely pleasurable emotion. It has a transforming impact on the individual. We will turn to a study of that impact and our reaction to it after we look at one final interpretation of religious experience.

### Abraham Maslow

So far we have studied analyses of religious experience by two theists, Otto and Buber, and a third person very sympathetic to theism but not clearly a theist himself, Jung. Now we turn our attention to a man who clearly rejects theism, yet seeks at the same time to exalt the values of religious experience. I speak of Abraham Maslow, recently deceased leader of the "third movement" in psychology—i.e., humanistic psychology as distinguished from Freudian psychology and behaviorist psychology. The quotations that follow will come from Maslow's book, *Religions, Values, and Peak-Experiences*.

According to Maslow the goal of humanistic psychology is twofold. It is to help each person become as *fully human* as possible—showing regard for the values of justice and compassion, and as *fully self-realized* as possible—searching out and actualizing his unique potentials as an individual. "In a word, it should help him to become the best he is capable of becoming, to become *actually* what he deeply is *potentially*."[42] The person who is solidly on the path to this goal is, in Maslow's terminology, a "self-actualizing individual." Unfortunately, there are many factors in our time that work against self-actualization, and the worst of these is *valuelessness*.[43] All the traditional systems of value in the West have been founded on theism and have claimed to be objectively authoritative because of the will of God; yet, as present circumstances testify, these systems have failed. Because many people have assumed—owing to Western tradition—that any value system claiming to be objective *must* be grounded on God, they have concluded—owing to the practical failures of theistic value systems and the increasing difficulties of believing in the biblical God at all—that the construction of an objective value system is impossible. Hence, along with the existence of God, they believe they have thrown out the possibility of an objective value system. But they haven't. Indeed, by throwing out the theistic God idea they have, perhaps without realizing it, created the social climate necessary for the construction of a truly objective, human system of values.

Our problem is to *construct* this new system, and we will be able to do that only if we do not fall victim again to the idea that values must be grounded on a concept of God. A system of values, Maslow argues, is too precious and urgent a thing to tie to so dubious a hypothesis as that of the existence of God. Our values must be grounded in Nature, for Nature is a *fact* rather than an hypothesis; it permits observation and control rather than requiring prayer and faith. Hence, what we need to do is to construct a set of values that is *confirmed by experience* and *useful in action.* Such values "we can believe in and devote ourselves to because they are *true* [italics mine] rather than because we are exhorted to 'believe and have faith.'"[44]

As a result of these convictions, Maslow spends time criticizing both conservative theists and liberal religionists. The *conservative* theists he criticizes for foisting on the world the belief that values must be grounded in or by God, or otherwise lose all authority. He argues that values are a *human* phenomenon which can be investigated, clarified, and justified without reference beyond the realm of nature.

Religious liberals are criticized for thinking that in throwing out theism, they also had to throw out the emotions of religious experience such as awe, reverence, humility, and adoration. They didn't have to do that. Yet they did. The result?

> A rather bleak, boring, unexciting, unemotional, cool philosophy of life which fails to do what the traditional religions have tried to do when they were at their best, to inspire, to awe, to comfort, to fulfill, to guide in the value choices, and to discriminate between higher and lower, better and worse, not to mention to produce Dionysiac experiences, wildness, rejoicing, impulsiveness.[45]

To be sure, a religion, any religion, should be "[1] intellectually credible and [2] morally worthy of respect, but it must also be [3] emotionally satisfying (and I include here," Maslow writes, "the transcendent emotions as well)."[46] Inasmuch as liberal religions neglect these emotions (which we will be examining more fully a few paragraphs hence), it is no surprise that they "exert so little influence even though their members are the most intelligent and most capable section of the population. It *must* be so," Maslow emphasizes, "just as long as they base themselves upon a lopsided picture of human nature which omits most of what human beings value, enjoy, and cherish in themselves, in fact, which they live for, and which they refuse to be done out of."[47]

If liberal churches *want* to exercise a broad and profound influence on individuals and their societies, then they must reclaim the values of religious experience for contemporary people and show that these values can be had without belief in God! This is an especially urgent task today, "because of the widespread 'valuelessness' in our society, i.e., people have nothing to admire, to sacrifice themselves for, to surrender to, to die for."[48] Why are they in this state? Because they have unfortunately and unnecessarily allowed themselves to be deprived of those emotions out of which our most basic values are formed—namely, the emotions of religious experience. To be sure, according to Maslow religious liberals did us a great service in leading the way from theism to atheism, but they did us a great disservice in thinking that they also had to abjure religious experience. As a consequence, we have been plunged into an era of meaninglessness, for it is in and from religious experiences that we derive our values! Without such experience we are sailors adrift on a starless night, with nothing to guide ourselves by. Fortunately, we needn't remain in this vacuum of values, for "When we are well and healthy and adequately fulfilling the concept 'human being,' then experiences of transcendence should in principle be commonplace."[49]

The experience of transcendence, Maslow contends, is the dynamic source of all the great religions. "The very beginning, the intrinsic core, the essence, the universal nucleus of every known high religion," he writes,

> . . . has been the private, lonely, personal illumination, revelation, or ecstasy of some acutely sensitive prophet or seer. The high religions call themselves revealed religions and each of them tends to rest its validity, its function, and its right to exist on the codification and the communication of this original mystic experience of revelation from the lonely prophet to the mass of human beings in general.[50]

This original revelation or mystical experience, which is transmitted from the solitary prophet to the masses, need not be interpreted in supernaturalistic terms. Rather, it "can be subsumed under the head of the 'peak-experiences' or 'ecstasies' or 'transcendent' experiences which are now eagerly investigated by many psychologists."[51] To be sure, on account of the prescientific world views of the cultures within which the classic "revelations" took place, it was natural and inevitable that they were interpreted as gifts from the supernatural. Today, however, we can see that those experiences were perfectly natural human experiences which can be examined scientifically. Hence, peak-experience, the core and dynamic source of religion, is an appropriate object of scientific examination and not something that lies beyond the realm of science. We shall return to this point after a fuller look at Maslow's description of peak-experience.

It might become tedious to tell you here all that Maslow has said about peak-experience (a term which he prefers to "religious experience" since it is broader and doesn't carry the theistic connotations which "religious experience" does), but it is important to lift up some of the basic characteristics that will help you understand how peak-experience can be the source of both religion and of our norms and values. In the first place, Maslow claims that everything Rudolf Otto defined as characteristic of religious experience can be enjoyed by the atheist as well as the theist:

> the holy; the sacred; creature feeling; humility; gratitude and oblation; thanksgiving; awe before the *mysterium tremendum;* the sense of the divine, the ineffable; the sense of littleness before mystery; the quality of exaltedness and sublimity; the awareness of limits and even of powerlessness; the impulse to surrender and to kneel; a sense of the eternal and of fusion with the whole of the universe; even the experience of heaven and hell.[52]

Next he claims that "in the peak-experience there is a very characteristic disorientation in time and space, or even the lack of consciousness of time and space. Phrased positively," he writes, "this is like experiencing universality and eternity."[53] Clearly, this kind of experience is radically different from ordinary experience. "The person in the peak-experiences may feel a day passing as if it were minutes or also a minute so intensely lived that it might feel like a day or a year or an eternity even. He may also lose his consciousness of being located in a particular place."[54]

In addition to being filled with the traditional emotions of religious experience and being characterized by disorientation in space and time, peak-experience is, thirdly, a type of experience in which

> the dichotomies, polarities, and conflicts of life tend to be transcended or resolved. That is to say, there tends to be a moving toward the perception of unity and integration in the world. The person himself tends to move toward fusion, integration, and unity and away from splitting, conflicts, and oppositions.[55]

Moveover, and fourthly, "In the peak-experiences, there tends to be a loss, even though transient, of fear, anxiety, inhibition, of defense and control, of perplexity, confusion, conflict, of delay and restraint. The profound fear of disintegration, of insanity, of death, all tend to disappear for the moment."[56] Consequently, peak-experiences frequently have a therapeutic effect and can have a profound and enduring transforming effect which amounts to a conversion.

Regarding the formation of our values, Maslow points out that we learn in the peak-experience that "joy, ecstasy, and rapture do in fact exist and that they are in principle available for the experiencer, even if they never have been before. Thus the peaker [the person who has a peak-experience] learns surely and certainly that life *can* be worthwhile, that it *can* be beautiful and valuable." He learns that there are things in life "which are so precious in themselves as to prove that not everything is a means to some end other than itself."[57] Some things are ends in themselves. Hence, the peak-experience does not stand in need of justification by means of something beyond itself. Why? Because it is "felt as a self-validating, self-justifying moment which carries its own intrinsic value with it. It is felt to be a highly valuable—even uniquely valuable—experience, so great an experience sometimes that even to attempt to justify it takes away from its dignity and worth."[58] Further, peak-experiences not only enrich life; in some instances they are responsible for its continuation. How so? By showing potential suicides that there *are* things worth living for—namely, peak-experiences themselves. Hence, once experienced, they refute the proposition that life is meaningless. They give the peaker something good to remember, to look forward to, and to enjoy.

The good news, according to Maslow, is that peak-experiences are available to *everyone*—and not to just a few mystics. Moreover, by means of scientific investigation, we can determine the type of people to whom such experiences come most frequently, the circumstances under which these experiences are most likely to occur, and how they might best be blended into our lives as a whole. This knowledge can then be generalized— by means of education and counseling—from those few people who are *natural* "peakers" to anyone who is interested in increasing the peak-experiences in his own life or the life of someone he cares about. Hence, our individual ability to cause peak-experiences whenever we desire will come increasingly under our control if we investigate them scientifically and develop the requisite conditions and discipline. Eventually, then, we might, whenever we desire, have all the blessings of religious experience without any of the problems caused by questionable creeds and dogmas.

Having spent so much time on peak-experience, a brief word is in order about *the nadir-experience* and *the plateau-experience*. The nadir-experience is simply the opposite of the peak-experience. It is as intense, but it is an experience of disharmony, of fragmentation, of desolation and emptiness. The plateau-experience, by contrast, is a positive rather than negative state of mind, but it lacks the intensity of either the peak-experience or the nadir-experience. It is "serene and calm, rather than a poignantly emotional, climactic" response to the awesome or miraculous.[59] Rather than being experienced as an explosion, it is "more often experienced as pure enjoyment and happiness, as, let's say, in a mother sitting quietly looking, by the hour, at her baby playing, and marveling, wondering, philosophizing, not quite believing. She can experience this as a very pleasant, continuing, contemplative experience rather than as something akin to a climactic explosion which then ends."[60] Happily, plateau-experiences are far easier to bring about by personal volition than are peak-experiences. "One can learn to see in this Unitive way almost at will. It then becomes a witnessing, an appreciating, what one might call a serene, cognitive blissfulness which can . . . have a quality of casualness and of lounging about."[61] Moreover, by means of thought, effort, and perseverance, we can achieve and maintain ourselves indefinitely in a state of plateau-experiencing. Hence, we can reach a point where we *stay* turned on by life. I once asked a perennially happy person why she was always so happy. Her reply? "I guess I'm just stoned on life!" That kind of experience isn't like the peak-experience of suddenly ascending a mountain top and just as suddenly descending. Rather, it's like *living* on a mountain top—and that's hard to beat.

One final note: Maslow is highly critical of religious institutions— churches, temples, etc.—for the extent to which they have ignored or suppressed peak-experience rather than encouraging and cultivating it. "Most people," he writes,

> lose or forget the subjectively religious experience, and redefine Religion as a set of habits, behaviors, dogmas, forms, which at the extreme becomes entirely legalistic and bureaucratic, conventional, empty, and in the truest meaning of the word, anti-religious.[62]

When this happens, a person's purported religion becomes a pseudo-religion and his deepest commitments switch elsewhere without his realization that his old religion has been superseded by a new one. A further aspect of this withering process is that "the mystic experience, the moment of illumination, the great awakening, along with the charismatic seer who started the whole thing, are forgotten, lost, or transformed into their opposites." Consequently, Maslow warns us that organized religions "finally may become the major enemies of the religious experience and the religious experiencer."[63]

What is your reaction to Maslow's warning? "Right on!"? He has pointed out a very real danger and we should heed it. Still, I believe there is also a grievous omission in his treatment of peak-experience. Specifically, he does not provide for the I–Thou type of religious experience Buber speaks of. Theists would say that that kind of experience is *the* religious experience *par excellence.* They would agree that Maslow's peak-experiences are a real and valuable kind of experience, but they simply do not include religious experience in the theistic sense. This is made especially clear by Maslow's claim that by means of scientific analysis, we can learn to *control* peak-experience. For surely if there is a supreme personal being, we will not be able to control that being in the least respect. Right? Further, such control is antithetical to a genuinely personal relationship, whether between God and person or person and person, for an authentic friendship is not achieved by control and manipulation. And because religious experience of the I–Thou type is the result of a *personal* relationship with God, a religious experience of the biblical sort must not be a peak-experience of Maslow's kind. Again, then, Maslow's treatment of peak-experience excludes what theists would consider the most important kind of "peak" experience.[64]

Moreover, if there is a God in the biblical sense, isn't anyone who takes Maslow's attitude toward peak-experiences—considering them all to be natural experiences subject to scientific analysis and control—cutting himself off from the possibility of developing a *personal* relationship with God? Why would that happen? Because the human person would assume that the feeling of the presence of a divine person is really only the result of natural forces—which he will seek to manipulate according to his wishes. Under such circumstances, it seems reasonable to assume that God would withdraw His presence. Wouldn't you?

Finally, the better part of wisdom seems to be to hold open the possibility of religious experience in the biblical sense. Why? Because if there *is* a God in the biblical sense, then considering what and who God is, and considering the testimony of theistic mystics as to the beauty of His presence, it would be contrary to our own deepest desires—if my analysis in Chapter 4 is basically correct—to cut ourselves off from His presence. And if there is *not* a God in the biblical sense, then nothing significant seems to be lost by not excluding from our world view the possibility of a theistic religious experience. Right?[65]

## THE MOMENT OF RESPONSE

To review quickly the cycle of religious growth, the first phase is the phase of the restless spirit, of the hungry heart, of *pursuit,* whereas the second phase is the phase of *revelation.* It is the moment during which something of supreme importance is discovered. That it is of supreme importance is not something which someone *tells* you. It is your *own* feeling during that moment. If your interpretation of the source of your revelation does not discredit it—by attributing it to a trick played on you by your mind, your body, your circumstances, another person, or an evil demon— then you are led to the third phase of the cycle of religious growth, namely, the phase of personal *response* to that which has been revealed. This phase consists of one's decision either to live according to that which has been revealed or to live irresponsibly toward it. I say "irresponsibly" because it was *one's own conviction* during the moment of revelation that what was revealed was something of supreme importance, something that should be honored in all the moments of one's life. Hence, if one does not honor it but neglects or betrays it, then—unless what was revealed has been surpassed in one's judgment by something yet greater—one is living irresponsibly toward it.

### Authenticity and Inauthenticity

This moment of decision is impossible before the moment of revelation, for then we are simply another animal, seeking to survive and to enjoy ourselves in the many ways made possible by our bodies and minds. Our lives then are lived wholly within the realms of physical, social, and cultural pleasures and pains. Søren Kierkegaard calls this "the aesthetic stage" of life. Human life at a higher level than this—at the levels Kierkegaard calls "the ethical stage" and "the religious stage" of life—cannot begin until we hunger and thirst after something more than the pleasures afforded by the senses, the mind, and society. The possibility of being fully human, or at least *more* fully human, comes only when our religious needs have been aroused and spoken to. After that moment we live either *authentically* or *inauthentically,* in *guilt* or in *good conscience*—for we either lead a life of devotion to that which has been revealed or we revert to a life oriented to the satisfaction of the body and the ego. We should distinguish, then, between human life before the moment of revelation and human life after that moment. Life before revelation can be no more than a life of *prudence in pursuit of survival and pleasure.* Life after revelation is either a life of *loyalty* or *disloyalty* to that which has been revealed. It is a life *unified* by revelation or *torn* by infidelity—but it can never again be life without a sense of something that is transcendently true and important. Hence, as well as being invited to "see and enjoy" in the moment of revelation, we are called to "hear and obey." I would like to expand on the nature and significance of this call by drawing on the insights of two contemporary thinkers, Philip Phenix and Abraham Heschel.[66]

### Philip Phenix: the Pleasant and the Sacred

Phenix, a professor of education at Columbia University, published a book in 1961 titled *Education and the Common Good.* In this book he draws out the profound difference between a life built on *desire (pursuit of the pleasant)* and a life built on *loyalty to the excellent (good, sacred).* Without presuming to tell us what "the good" is, Phenix points out that we do each have experiences of the good. Moreover, he claims, our experience is such that we feel that the good is something objective, something that has authority over us, and not something that is merely a whim of our desires or a figment of our imagination. In our moments of religious experience, of revelation, we are convinced that what is revealed to us is not merely expedient for the moment, but is what we ought to honor at all times—whether it be to our worldly advantage or not. The sacred is not *whatever* we will, but that which *we* feel in our depths we *ought* to will. It is not our creation. It is our Creator—if we let it be. It is that which creates meaning, unity, and direction in our lives. Our experience, then, is always that the sacred possesses a validity apart from our whims and wishes. It seizes us and convicts us. It is that perfect combination of the good and the right. It cannot be equated with pleasure. Devotion to the sacred is fundamentally different from desire for pleasure. The former is other-regarding whereas the latter is self-interested. Devotion "entails sacrifice and loyalty instead of conferring gratification and comfort. It is concerned with giving instead of getting."[67]

Now you might be thinking, à la Ayn Rand, critic of altruism and author of *The Virtue of Selfishness,* "I'll be damned if I'm going to sacrifice my good times to the Good, the Right, the Sacred, or anything else!" The problem, of course, is that human happiness cannot be found in pleasure. Phenix is only inviting you to abandon an *illusory* source of happiness. After the moment of revelation, pleasure is no longer enough for us because we have become aware of a dimension of reality that transcends the pleasant, evoking worship, devotion, and adoration. It is through awareness of that dimension of reality and through loyalty to that which is revealed within it that we grow in beauty of character, unity of purpose, strength of will, and peace of mind. To live a life of loyalty does not mean to lose the will or capacity to enjoy social, intellectual, and bodily pleasures, but it does mean the discovery that these sources of pleasure do not deserve top priority. It involves the discovery that when the hard choice comes between pursuit of pleasure and pursuit of excellence, our lives, paradoxically, are less impoverished and more ennobled if we choose excellence and sacrifice pleasure. Phenix makes this point in the following words: "The history of mankind and the facts of personal experience suggest that the health and fulfillment of life spring from *release from self-centeredness in loyalty to the good.*"[68] Also, "The fulfillment of personal existence comes not from grasping for it, but . . . as a by-product of self-forgetful and loving devotion to the good."[69]

Once we have become sensitive to the sacred as it is revealed in our lives, what we do on our own initiative, out of our own heads, may prove temporarily interesting, but it will never prove deeply satisfying. Its shallowness will become more and more dissatisfying until we seal ourselves off in a neurosis or begin to take the sacred seriously. It need not always be the case, of course, that what we desire and what is of worth be at variance with one another. A healthy religion affirms that these two things, the desired and the excellent, are not always the same—since sometimes we desire that which is unworthy or wrong; yet it attempts to put us in touch with that which can mold our desires so that we desire the excellent and are enabled to pursue it in spite of threats, distractions, and inertia. To be transformed in this way does not destroy our ability to enjoy the pleasurable. It only leads us to give it a lower priority, so that instead of seeking fulfillment through self-centered striving for pleasure, possessions, power, and applause, we find our fulfillment in loyalty to the sacred. Phenix should quite agree, then, with Carl Jung's statement that "man's life should be sacrificial, that is, offered up to an idea greater than man," for only in this way shall human fulfillment be found.[70] And ultimately, I add in the spirit of St. Anselm, we should give ourselves to "that than which nothing greater can be conceived."

### Abraham Heschel: Faith as Faithfulness

Phenix, as far as I know, is not a theist but a naturalist—i.e., he believes that Nature is the whole of reality. Abraham Heschel, recently deceased professor of theology at the Jewish Theological Seminary in New York City, was a deeply theistic Jew. Yet in spite of their differences in philosophical orientation, Phenix and Heschel disclose basically similar understandings of the nature of the religious life. Again, as with Tillich and Fromm, my intuitions are that such a fundamental agreement between people writing from such different perspectives is probably the result of the facts imposing themselves, rather than of sheer coincidence. To be sure, there are profound differences between Phenix and Heschel, though we won't focus on these. Neither shall I discuss their similarities, for I believe these will impress themselves upon you as I simply relate some basic points from two of Heschel's books, *Man Is Not Alone* and *God in Search of Man*.

Heschel emphasizes the ephemerality of the moment of revelation and he states that *"faith is faithfulness,* loyalty to an event, loyalty to our response.'' His approach to this definition is as follows:

> Authentic faith is more than an echo of a tradition. It is a creative situation, an event. For God is not always silent, and man is not always blind. In every man's life there are moments when there is a lifting of the veil at the horizon of the known, opening a sight of the eternal. Each of us has at least once in his life experienced the momentous reality of God. Each of us has once caught a glimpse of the beauty, peace and power that flow through the souls of those who are devoted to Him. But such experiences or inspirations are rare events. To some people they are like shooting stars, passing and unremembered. In others they kindle a light that is never quenched. The remembrance of that experience and the loyalty to the response of that moment are the forces that sustain our faith. In this sense, faith is faithfulness, loyalty to an event, loyalty to our response.[71]

I must admit that I was puzzled at first by Heschel's description of faith as "loyalty to our response"—perhaps you are too. I think what he means—and he has an important point—is that the moment of revelation is *defined* in part by the wholeheartedness of our response, by our *feeling* that *we are* apprehending that which is true and right and good and holy. Faith is loyalty to and trust of the response that we had in the moment of revelation, a response of commitment, of wholehearted allegiance. In our less exalted, more mundane, even depressed, moments, we should neither lose sight of what we felt in the moment of revelation nor betray it. Rather, we should self-consciously guide our lives by it. In brief, we should be loyal to our response during that moment, for it represents our own deepest and clearest sentiments as to what is right and good and true.

Regarding the ephemerality of the moment of revelation, Heschel writes in *God in Search of Man,* "The immediate certainty that we attain in moments of insight does not retain its intensity after the moments are gone."[72] Hence, to borrow a phrase from Archibald MacLeish's *J.B.,* religion becomes a matter of blowing on the coals of the heart—that we might not lose their warmth altogether and that they might burst into flame once again. In between these moments of religious conflagration the problem of the religious person is "how to communicate those rare moments of insight to all the hours of our life? How to commit intuition to concepts, the ineffable to words, insight to rational understanding? How to convey our insights to others and to unite in a fellowship of faith?"[73] Why make the effort to do these things? Because "great events, just as great works of art, are significant in themselves. Our interest in them endures long after they are gone."[74] Hence, we should sound our lives for our personal peak-experiences and we should sound human history for its peak experiences, in order that they might become our own. As Karl Jaspers puts it, "It is by such moments and for such moments that we live."[75]

### *The Way of Greece and the Way of Israel*

When Heschel talks about "great events" he clearly has in mind the great events of the history of Israel, such as the exodus from Egypt and the delivery of the commandments to Moses on Mount Sinai. An atheist could also have a list of what he considers the most significant events in history and he could orient his life by them. Hence, what I shall call "the way of Israel" is not limited to theists, but it is, I think, profoundly different from what I shall call "the way of Greece." "The way of Israel" is to guide oneself by concrete events in human history and in one's personal life. Concepts are of secondary importance in this way and are used to unpack the meaning and richness of such events as the Exodus or Gandhi's march to the sea or Hitler's fascist regime. "The way of Greece," on the other hand, the way that is most commonly associated with philosophers, whether correctly or not, is to guide oneself by means of timeless concepts abstracted from reality. The concrete events of human history and of one's personal life are here subordinate to concepts, in the sense that the former provide the data from which one moves by means of reason toward a *conception* of the real and the good. It is then the concept, rather than the event, by which one guides one's life. To the Israelite, by contrast, *events* are always richer than concepts, and *history* is the stage on which the good and the real are revealed. To the Greek, events are grist for the mill of *reason*, which *abstracts* from them, or sees *through* them, the truth about the real and the good. Hence, his objective is to transcend history by grasping timeless truths.

The Israelite and the Greek agree that concepts and events are both necessary to human existence. They disagree as to which should be subordinate to the other. What do you think? Should we orient our lives primarily by means of events or of concepts? Which way do you tend to go? Is there a third way? Perhaps "the way of India," that is, of mysticism which transcends concepts and events? I have made the distinction for you between "the way of Israel" and "the way of Greece" because I believe these two ways are characteristic of two large groups of people who perceive the world in fundamentally different ways and who, for that reason, have a great deal of difficulty appreciating and communicating with one another. Which group do you belong to, if either? Can you think of people who, in your opinion, clearly belong in one group or the other? Is one way superior to the other as a philosophy of life? How so? Is each way superior to the other in some respects but inferior in others? Can you explain the differences?

## THE STAGE OF ACTION

Whereas the third phase of the cycle of religious growth consists of the *decision* to live for that which has been revealed to us or to neglect or betray it, the fourth phase consists of our *living out a positive decision* to be loyal to that which has been revealed. Whereas the moment of decision (which is never settled once and for all but must be confronted again and again) is subjective and internal, the stage of action is objective and external, for in it what we have decided flows out into our daily lives. Primarily, I believe, the phase of action will express itself in *worship* and in *work*. Let's look more closely at each of these.

### Worship

Most of us are familiar with worship as an activity which people engage in on a certain day, at a certain time, in a certain place. What is that activity all about? Ideally, worship is that activity during which we self-consciously focus our attention on the sacred in as clear and whole-hearted a manner as possible. A full act of worship has various aspects which we will look at shortly, but first it is worth noting that worship is something which cannot be done mechanically or perfunctorily. Participation in a service of worship, when that participation is sincere, is never a mere repetition of words and acts one has learned at church, temple or elsewhere. A person who is merely going through the motions is no more worshipping than a robot that is going through the same motions and making the same sounds. Worship requires subjective as well as outward participation.

Regarding its various aspects, worship at its fullest is that activity during which we *recall* those moments of revelation which represent the high points of our awareness. Affirmations of faith, readings of religious literature, performance of rituals, and singing of hymns are all ways of recollecting these high points, of dilating the inner eye so that the divine light might flood in again with its original intensity and clarity. "Praise," "Thanksgiving," and "Adoration" are all traditional parts of a Judeo-Christian worship service during which the high points of the tradition are remembered. Through worship we also *reappropriate* the meaning and significance of the sacred as it has been revealed to us. We reappropriate it in order to *make mid-flight corrections* in the directions our lives are taking, and in order that we might *regain perspective* on our lives as a whole, so as not to be crushed in the welter of demands, temptations, distractions, and tragedies that bombard us from time to time, and sometimes from moment to moment. Such reappropriation is assisted in some traditions by the taking of sacraments, the performance of rites, and "the hearing of the word." Many Catholics, for example, receive the sacrament of Holy Communion every Sunday. Each Sunday Protestants hear sermons that apply some portion of the Bible to contemporary personal and social problems. Muslims around the world daily perform the perspective-inducing act of praying five times facing Mecca: upon rising, at noon, during mid-afternoon, at sunset, and before evening sleep. Clearly, these all are efforts not only to *recall* the sacred, but to *reappropriate* it.

Having recalled and re-encountered the sacred, worship is also understandably that activity during which we face up honestly to the *gap* between our sense of the sacred and our behavior. Hence, in Judeo-Christian services of worship there are opportunities for "confession" of sins and "petition" of God's mercy and forgiveness. At this time we may also seek the strength and the transforming power to narrow the gap and eventually to close it, so that our thoughts, words, and actions come into complete harmony with our sense of the sacred. Next in worship, though not necessarily in this order, we open ourselves to *new* revelations or inspirations. Some religious groups, such as Unitarian-Universalists, open themselves to inspiration from every religious tradition, whereas others look only to the religious tradition to which they belong. Some persons expect *new revelations,* in the sense of new *truths* about reality. Others believe that the old revelations will not be added to but that we can expect new *inspirations,* in the sense of deeper *insights* into the meaning, truth, and relevance of the original revelations. In every case, though, there is in worship an openness to, expectation of, and desire for new and fresh contact with the sacred. Finally, worship is an activity that *issues into everyday life*—reminding us of its ideal possibilities and sending us to invest our lives in the actualization of those possibilities. This leads us quite naturally to the topic of *work.*

### Work

I claimed at the beginning of this section that the fourth phase of religious growth, the phase of action, expresses itself in worship and in work. I have spoken at length about worship, but there is little I can say about work as a natural expression of religious commitment. It does seem implicit in the revelatory moment that we *act* in whatever ways we can to transform ourselves and the world in the direction of our vision of the good. The form our work should take, however, must be a highly individual matter depending upon the *content* of our personal revelations and the *circumstances* of our lives. Albert Schweitzer, who at age thirty abandoned a brilliant career in music and theology to become a medical missionary, is very careful in his autobiography, *Out of My Life and Thought,* to point out that people should not assume that his type of radical change is the path for all to follow. Some people feel that they must make a drastic career change in order to honor their sense of the sacred, but for most of us, I suspect, our religious work lies in sanctifying our everyday relationships and in solving problems close to home. In either case, there is plenty of work for each of us, work whereby we can achieve a sense of significant participation in the ongoing creation of the world.

### Is Pleasure Always Our Motive?

Keeping in mind the necessary eventuation of religious action in work as well as worship, but respecting the highly personal nature of the form that one's work takes, let's turn to an examination of some further questions about worship. In Chapter 5, during our examination of the humanistic aspect of a healthy religion, I referred with approval to Whitehead's claim that enjoyment is the purpose of life and to Steinberg's claim that we have a God-given duty to enjoy our existence. But can a life of worship, in the sense of *self-conscious devotion to the sacred,* be reconciled with a life of enjoyment? Ideally, worship and enjoyment shall be *combined.* Clearly, however, these two can come into conflict, and just as clearly, whenever they do come into conflict, we should choose worship rather than enjoyment. You may be thinking, "There's really no difference. People do only what they enjoy. Hence, if we choose to worship rather than to play golf, or whatever, it is only because we *enjoy* worshipping more than we enjoy these other things. Pleasure is our goal all along; it just takes a different form for the saint than for the sensualist." Personally, I don't agree with this analysis. It seems to me that there is a significant difference between worship and indulgence. Commitment to the sacred, for example, may entail sacrifice and discomfort. You might reply, "But pursuit of pleasure might also involve sacrifice and discomfort, for sometimes we must sacrifice small pleasures now for the sake of large pleasures later, and sometimes we must endure discomfort now, such as physical exercise or dieting, in order to receive accolades later." That's true. The pursuit of pleasure can entail sacrifice and discomfort. However, such sacrifice and discomfort is *for the sake of eventual pleasure.* If the anticipated pleasure is not forthcoming, we are free to abstain from further discomfort or sacrifice, for the latter were assumed solely as *means* to the former. Hence, our choice of a path to pleasure is always a matter of prudence, since if pleasure doesn't follow as anticipated, we are under no obligation to continue on that path. We are free to do whatever else gives greater promise of effectiveness.

Worship, to the contrary, is not *for* the sake of eventual pleasure. If it were, and if the anticipated pleasure were not forthcoming, we would be free to cease worshipping. But we are not. Commitment to the sacred is not a matter of expediency. Hence, it is fundamentally different from the pursuit of pleasure. Indeed, pleasure—large or small, now or later—is to be sacrificed whenever it would interfere with one's sense of harmony with the right and the good. You could say, "But that is because a feeling of harmony with the right and the good is the most pleasant of all feelings," and I don't know how to reply to that except to say that it seems strange to say that a person who dies a death by torture for the sake of convictions, and without knowing whether there is life after death, is acting for the sake of pleasure. You might concede, "Okay, such a person is not acting for the sake of pleasure in the ordinary sense. Rather, he is seeking to avoid pain—namely, the pain of the guilt he would incur if he betrayed his sense of the sacred." This is closer to the truth, I think, yet it doesn't ring completely true either, for a martyr's intention is not necessarily the attainment of pleasure or the avoidance of pain. It may simply be unflinching testimony to that which he finds most precious. By his courageous suffering he is not attempting to achieve an ecstatic experience or avoid excruciating guilt. He is simply trying to preserve his relationship to the sacred—a relationship which is not always the most pleasant, but which is always the most important.

Inasmuch as our relationship to the sacred is the most important relationship in our lives, the most important thing we can do is to discern the sacred as it is revealed in our lives and then to live our lives according to it. If we are very fortunate, we will be able both to honor our sense of the sacred and to enjoy our existence. Perhaps this combination is what makes the idea of heaven so powerful—for it is difficult, and some would say impossible, to live in this world both a worshipful life and a life of enjoyment. This is not because religiousness frowns on pleasure. It doesn't. Rather, it is because it so often calls us away from innocent enjoyment to fight injustice, starvation, and other social ills. Immanuel Kant, one of the great modern philosophers, held that the supreme good for human beings is the combination of virtue and happiness. He understood virtue to be the practice of doing what is morally right *because* it is morally right. Only the virtuous, those who honor and obey their sense of what is morally right, *deserve* happiness, he reasoned. But they rarely receive it on earth. Indeed, as we noted above, their obedience to morality often deprives them of pleasure and afflicts them with suffering. Still, they, and not the immoral, *deserve* happiness, so Kant held to a firm hope that there will be a life after death in which the virtuous are rewarded with happiness. Surely the hope of heaven, for those who hold it, is an incentive for sacrificing pleasure to the sacred, since the pleasure being sacrificed now is *transient,* whereas honoring the sacred, it is believed, is rewarded with *eternal* pleasure. But what about those who believe that life after death is not even a possibility? Why should *they* sacrifice pleasure to the sacred? (You might want to pause to think about that. I won't attempt an answer here.)

### When Worship?

Now let me ask another question: Do you think we should worship only when we feel like it? (Please don't read on until you've clarified your feelings and your reasons on this point.)

Most of the people to whom I have put this question believe that we should worship only when we feel like it. I disagree because it seems to me that the very logic of the moment of revelation and of our affirmative response is that we should not worship only when we feel like it. Why? Because the feeling we have *during* the moment of revelation is that we are experiencing something which is significant for *every* moment of life, something which we want always to keep freshly and clearly in the center of consciousness—and what is worship but an attempt to *recapture* the impact of earlier revelatory moments and to keep ourselves *open* to new ones— keeping aglow the coals of the heart till they burst into flame again? Hence, the nature of the revelatory moment and of our own best judgment during that moment obliges us to bring ourselves regularly back under the influence of that moment so that we do not lose its perspective and so that our lives do not fall below the new height it has lifted us to. It would seem, then, that to worship only "when the spirit moves us" is contrary to the content of the revelatory moment and is, therefore, incompatible with living a fully religious life. Right?

If I am correct about the relation of worship to the revelatory moments of our lives, then I think you can see the criteria by which the content and structure of services of worship should be—and probably have been—determined for the most part. Since the purpose of a service of worship, broadly speaking, is to recover and respond to the content of revelation, therefore the music, rituals, symbols, prayers, creeds, readings, sermons, dances, architecture, and other elements of worship and its supporting context—not that all people use all of these elements—should be constructed and used at such times and in such ways that they capture accurately our past response to revelation and effectively help us regain that response in a deep and moving way—and perhaps help some gain it for the first time. The next time you attend a worship service you might reflect on the ways in which its rituals, symbols, music, prayers, and so on contribute to the expression and recovery of a sense of the sacred. You might be concerned that to do such a thing would require that you take the point of view of an outsider, such as a sociologist visiting and observing the parts of the service and their coherence with one another. That is a danger you would run into if you put too much distance between yourself and what is going on in the service. But it is also possible, I think, to participate sincerely in a service and observe these things. Indeed, it can be a new and powerful experience to continue participating in a service while at the same time taking a larger point of view from which you consider yourself as one person among others participating in a certain context in a common act of worship. Such reflections can help us both to appreciate more fully and deeply what it is we are involved in and to become aware of ways in which what we are doing can be made more effective.

### Worship Together or Alone?

Finally, I raise for your consideration the question whether we should worship together or alone. Whitehead, you recall, said that religion is what we do with our *solitariness,* not our *togetherness.* So, we might ask, *why* worship together? Indeed, if religion is so private a thing as Maslow's peaker claims, how *can* we worship together? Is it really possible except in some empty formal sense?

I'm not as ready to answer these questions as I have been earlier ones. I do recall a young woman who told me that when she worships with her friends in their free-spirited Pentecostal manner, she feels that they lift one another to higher and higher heights by means of their spontaneous succession of songs, prayers, Bible readings, and personal sharing. Enhancement of one's worship experience (and enhancing the worship experience of others) certainly seems like a legitimate reason for worshipping with others. But perhaps "enhancement" is too shallow a word to convey what really goes on in group worship. As the "social construction of reality approach" might put it: in that social activity known as worship, it may be true that for those who are already initiated into the rites of the group, the worship experience is merely enhanced, but for those who are new to the group, such as children and outsiders, it is *by means of group worship* that the religious mode of consciousness is created in the first place. The religious mode of consciousness seems to be no more natural to human beings than to cats or any other creature. It is a social phenomenon—generated, sustained, and evolved by social processes. This is not necessarily to say that the creation of religious consciousness is an entirely human affair. Judaism and Christianity both affirm the corporate nature of their respective institutions, Israel and the Church. But though they are committed to different religious institutions, Jews and Christians generally agree that anyone who voluntarily remains outside the religious community will wither like an uprooted vine. They are agreed that spiritual nourishment comes ultimately from a personal God, but they are also agreed that it is mediated to us primarily through the community of the faithful. And for those people who do not believe in a divine being, the religious community becomes *all the more important* in the creation, maintenance, and advancement of religious consciousness!

To be sure, a religious community could spawn people who are then able as individuals to nourish their faith apart from the community. But if these people value their faith—and if they didn't they wouldn't nourish it—then their refusal to participate in a religious community would seem to show either ignorance or ingratitude: ignorance of the source from which they derived their "great treasure," as Jung calls it, or ingratitude toward that source. Knowledge of the source would seem to occasion gratitude, and gratitude would seem to call for some kind of a constructive response to religious community (though one may, in spite of gratitude, desire to reform one's religious community or even to change to another community that is closer to one's ideal). Finally, if one values greatly his religious faith, then normally he would want to transmit that value to others—such as children or adult seekers. Transmission of such a value would probably be achieved more effectively within a religious community than in a strictly one-to-one relationship. Again, then, participation in a religious community seems to be called for, and especially if one believes that being part of a community is part of what it means to be religious!

Regarding the belief that community is a part of being religious, discussion seems to be in order, so let's pursue it briefly. As the revelatory moment unifies the individual and gives direction to him, it might also unify individuals *with one another* and give direction to them *as a social whole*. In this case, people would be united by the *best* that they know (by their sense of the sacred), rather than by the *worst* (such as fear, greed, bigotry, or chauvinism). The question we seem to come back to here is whether *human solidarity* is implicit in the revelatory moment—and that is a question you and I can answer only on the basis of our individual revelatory experiences. If we do both believe that the ideal of human solidarity was implicit in our revelatory moments, then it would seem to follow that at certain intervals we should join together with one another and, to whatever extent is feasible, with all those who share our faith. Why? In order that we might express, celebrate, and deepen our solidarity with one another, and in order that we might join forces in behalf of our common ideals. If human solidarity is implicit in our revelatory moments, then perhaps Martin Buber is correct that *the best way to serve God is to build community.* Do you agree? Is the pursuit of human solidarity implicit in your sense of the sacred? If so, what concrete steps should (must?) be taken to honor it?

## THE CYCLE BEGINS AGAIN

If we do live out our lives as best we can according to our sense of the sacred, we will almost certainly discover that we still have unanswered questions and unsatisfied needs—some of them having been generated by our very effort to be faithful! Such needs and questions bring us full circle back to the stage of pursuit, which we hope will be followed by new events of revelation. Hence, the cycle begins again. That it begins again does not mean necessarily that we have been losing ground and now must regain it. Nor does its renewal mean a monotonous repetition of earlier cycles. It involves newness, and therefore growth. It is a spiral, and not just a cycle. It is something that has been going on since infancy, that reached self-consciousness in adolescence, and that, we hope, will reach maturity—though not fixity—in adulthood. Ideally the spiral of our religious growth will never stop until we have reached a religious position that is completely and enduringly satisfying. This does not mean that we should goad ourselves to uncover every imperfection in our present religion and then to agonize over each imperfection in order to hasten our journey to a perfect religion. That seems to me only a short way to misery—for those closest to us as well as ourselves. Rather, it means that we should *be honest* with ourselves and others about the deficiencies of our religion, or our understanding of it, and that we should *stay open* to and eager for further religious growth—whether such growth takes us further into our present religious direction or off into a radically new direction. Why stay honest and open? Because we want the best that there is. If what we already have *is* the best that there is, then—given an equal chance—it should come out on top in spite of criticisms leveled at it and alternatives proposed to it. If it is not the best, then it should be transcended. "Best" in what sense? In the sense of satisfying us personally in all the dimensions of our existence as creatures who are intellectual, emotional, and actual.

"And about the spiral of religious growth. There seems to be nothing systematic about the loops. They jiggle a lot and sometimes go twang. And there is a loop of faith hopefully in one's early childhood which is very large and unbending upon which the whole crazy wonderful spring rests."

Harriet Cramton

## Footnotes

1. All quotations from the Bible, unless noted otherwise, are from the Revised Standard Version of the Bible. Copyright 1952 and Copyright 1946, by Division of Christian Education of the National Council of Churches of Christ in the United States of America.

2. For an introduction to Zen Buddhism and its rejection of the Western attempt to satisfy spiritual yearning by means of reason or revelation, see chap. 1, "The Sense of Zen," in D. T. Suzuki's *Zen Buddhism,* William Barrett, ed. (New York: Doubleday and Company, Inc., 1956). This is an essay no Westerner should miss. Suzuki is the foremost interpreter of Zen to the West, and his essay, which appeared originally in his *Essays in Zen Buddhism, First Series* (New York: Paragon Book Reprint Corporation, 1971. Repr. of 1927 ed.), has been reprinted in many different volumes.

3. Carl G. Jung, *Modern Man in Search of a Soul,* trans. W. S. Dell and Cary F. Baynes (New York: Harcourt, Brace & World, Inc., 1933), p. 240.

4. John Dewey, in *A Common Faith* (New Haven: Yale University Press, 1934), takes the opposite position from Otto and explains religious experience as a form of other kinds of experience, such as were just mentioned in the text.

5. Rudolf Otto, *The Idea of the Holy,* trans. John W. Harvey (New York: Oxford University Press, 1958), p. 14.

6. Ibid., p. 20.

7. Ibid., p. 24.

8. Ibid., p. 25.

9. Ibid., p. 26.

10. Ibid., p. 28.

11. Ibid., p. 29.

12. Ibid., p. 30.

13. My story is freely adapted from the *Brihadaranyaka Upanishad.* There the dialogue is between a sage and his king, rather than father and son, and the things pointed to are the physical, mental, and vital aspects of reality, rather than a chair and a dog. None of these things is Brahman, either individually or taken together, but each of them points to Brahman, who transcends and includes them all.

14. Otto, *The Idea of the Holy,* p. 31.

15. Ibid., pp. 31–32.

16. Ibid., p. 33.

17. Ibid., p. 36.

18. Martin Buber, *Eclipse of God* (New York: Harper & Row, Publishers, 1952), p. 44.

19. For an introduction to Blaise Pascal, see Chap. 1 of David E. Roberts' *Existentialism and Religious Belief.* For a provocative intellectual and emotional experience, read Pascal's *Pensées* in his *Pensées* and *The Provincial Letters,* trans. W. F. Trotter and Thomas M'Crie (New York: Random House, Inc., 1941).

20. Dewey, *A Common Faith,* p. 42.

21. Buber, *Eclipse of God,* pp. 44–45.

22. Pascal, *Pensées,* p. 386.

23. To go more deeply into these issues would require a preliminary study of two metaphysical positions, materialism and idealism, and two epistemological positions, realism and phenomenalism. Many "Introduction to Philosophy" books treat all four topics; or see the appropriate selections in *The Encyclopedia of Philosophy,* Paul Edwards ed. (New York: Macmillan Publishing Company, 1967), 8 vols.

24. Buber, *Eclipse of God,* p. 28.

25. Ibid., p. 32.

26. Ibid., pp. 32–33. Italics mine.

27. A good introduction to Sartre is his own *Existentialism and Human Emotions* (New York: Philosophical Library, Inc., 1957). Sartre's major philosophical treatise is *Being and Nothingness* (New York: Washington Square Press, 1946), in addition to which he has written numerous plays, such as *No Exit* and *The Devil and the Good Lord.* Parenthetically, there are many modern people who testify that God is not silent in their lives. The extent to which people in the last quarter of the twentieth century feel that there is or is not a living God is a matter for sociologists to determine by sound research, not for philosophers to infer from a very narrow, highly personal range of evidence.

28. Buber, *Eclipse of God,* p. 23.

29. Ibid., p. 68.

30. Ibid., p. 36.

31. Ibid., pp. 36–37.

32. Jung, *Modern Man in Search of a Soul,* p. 229.

33. For an introduction to the work of Jung and many other leading psychologists, see *Theories of Personality,* 2nd ed., Calvin S. Hall and Gardner Lindzey (New York: John Wiley and Sons, Inc., 1970).

34. Jung, *Psychology and Religion* (New Haven: Yale University Press, 1938), p. 5.

35. Ibid., p. 4.

36. Ibid., p. 6.

37. Ibid., p. 37.

38. Ibid., p. 75.

39. Ibid., p. 98.

40. Professor Michael Meilach, O.F.M., has pointed out to me that the failure of a god to any longer empower a person may be the result of the person allowing or causing his relationship to that god to deteriorate. Hence, before abandoning a god, one should question seriously whether it is the god or oneself who is failing. A person who is going deaf may wonder why the bells toll ever more softly.

41. Jung, *Psychology and Religion,* pp. 113–114.

42. Abraham H. Maslow, *Religions, Values, and Peak-Experiences* (New York: The Viking Press, 1964), p. 49. This and other quotations from *Religions, Values, and Peak-Experiences* are used by permission of Kappa Delta Pi, an Honor Society in Education, owners of the copyright, P.O. Box A, West Lafayette, Indiana 47906.

43. See also Maslow's preface to *New Knowledge in Human Values,* edited by Maslow himself (New York: Harper & Row, Publishers, 1959).

44. Maslow, *Religions,* p. 83.

45. Ibid., p. 42.

46. Ibid., p. 43.

47. Ibid. Rev. Jack Taylor, himself a liberal religionist who is sympathetic to Maslow's emphasis on religious experience, remarked to me that Maslow has failed to appreciate the profoundly emotional experiences liberal religion has afforded its adherents by virtue of its emphasis on social action. Consider, for example, the emotional experiences religious liberals must have undergone when they marched on Washington in the sixties and heard Martin Luther King, Jr.'s, oration, "I Have A Dream," or when they joined hands in Selma, Alabama, and waded into a sea of hostility and violence that took the lives of two people, one a young liberal minister. It does appear that Maslow has neglected something important here.

48. Ibid., p. 42.

49. Ibid., p. 32. The practical problem, of course, is how to restore ourselves to a state of health. For a full statement of Maslow's prescription, see his *Motivation and Personality,* 2nd ed. (New York: Harper & Row, Publishers, 1970), or more recently, *Toward A Psychology of Being,* 2nd ed. (New York: Van Nostrand Reinhold Company, 1968).

50. Maslow, *Religions,* p. 19.

51. Ibid., pp. 19–20.

52. Ibid., p. 54.

53. Ibid., p. 63.

54. Ibid.

55. Ibid., pp. 65–66.

56. Ibid., p. 66.

57. Ibid., p. 75.

58. Ibid., p. 62.

59. Ibid., p. xiv.

60. Ibid., p. xv.

61. Ibid., p. xiv–xv.

62. Ibid., p. viii.

63. Ibid.

64. Paul Tillich has an important and pertinent passage on the nature of personal relationships in his *Biblical Religion and the Search for Ultimate Reality* (Chicago: The University of Chicago Press, 1955), pt. IV, sec. 1. See also Martin Buber's *I and Thou,* trans. Walter Kaufmann (New York: Charles Scribner's Sons, 1970).

65. The classic version of this "wager" type argument is by Blaise Pascal. See his *Pensées,* sec. 3, esp. no. 233. Whereas he emphasizes the negative reason for wagering one way rather than the other, I have emphasized the positive.

66. For valuable reflections on the nature and significance of fidelity, see Gabriel Marcel's *Creative Fidelity,* trans. Robert Rosthal (New York: Farrar, Straus, and Giroux, Inc., 1964), chap. 8, and his *Homo Viator: Introduction*

*to a Metaphysic of Hope,* trans. Emma Craufurd (New York: Harper & Row, Publishers, 1962), chap. v. Also, Sam Keen's *Gabriel Marcel* (Richmond, Va.: John Knox Press, 1967), pp. 34–40.

67. Philip H. Phenix, *Education and the Common Good* (New York: Harper & Brothers, 1961), p. 25.

68. Ibid., p. 26. Italics mine.

69. Ibid., p. 8.

70. Jung, *Psychology and Religion,* p. 94.

71. Abraham Heschel, *Man Is Not Alone* (New York: Harper & Row, Publishers, 1966), p. 65.

72. Heschel, *God in Search of Man* (New York: Harper & Row, Publishers, 1966), p. 132.

73. Ibid., p. 163.

74. Ibid., p. 211.

75. Karl Jaspers, *The Perennial Scope of Philosophy* (Hamden, Conn.: Archon Books, 1968), p. 73.

# Conclusion

- What is the difference between the "experimental" attitude toward a commitment and the "religious" attitude?
- What is W. C. Smith's distinction between *faith* and *cumulative tradition?*
- How does Smith's distinction help show that religious faith is inevitably personalized?
- What is a sad irony of religious education? How can it be overcome?
- What is Richard Rubenstein's recommendation regarding religious education?
- What are the three most radically different religious positions you can think of? What makes them so different?
- What are the main strengths and weaknesses of this book?
- Where do you go from here?

## THE EXPERIMENTAL ATTITUDE
## AND THE RELIGIOUS ATTITUDE


Throughout this book I have emphasized that the individual should determine his religious commitment out of the depths of his own experience and reflection. Now I would like to make a distinction lest you conclude that I believe that a mature religious faith is a calculating, selfish kind of thing that is constructed for the sake of achieving peace of mind, mystical ecstasy, heaven, or something else. The experimental attitude is appropriate when we are trying to figure out the best means to an end: we try this and that, use the best means available, but stand ready to discard it at any time. After all, it's just a means. It is the end that is important.

A mature religious faith, by contrast, is not in my opinion an experimental affair in the sense that we pick and choose our religious beliefs and objects of devotion according to how well they suit us. Rather, an object of religious devotion chooses us, compels us, convicts us. Religious faith is *not* a matter of experiment, but of *submission*—an idea captured nicely in the name of the religion established through Mohammed: "Islam" means "submission," and a Muslim is "one who submits." To be religious, I am suggesting, is not to choose but to submit. I would not recommend blind submission, as you know; but neither would I recommend submission with an ulterior purpose. That would not be sincere submission. What I do recommend and what I believe is actually at the heart of all sincere religious faith is *personal submission to the best that one knows.* The word "submission" has unfortunate connotations of servility which I do not mean to imply. Mature submission in a religious sense would consist of acknowledgement through thought, word, and deed of the sacred as it has been revealed to the individual. This kind of submission, it seems to me, ennobles the individual and deserves admiration.

It is true that by *living* according to our sense of the sacred, we discover the riches *and the deficiences* of that which has been revealed to us, and that in view of these deficiencies, we may seek a more adequate sense of the sacred. But if we live according to our sense of the sacred *in order* to discover its riches and deficiencies, then we have abandoned the attitude of religious commitment and are acting out of a self-gratifying motive. We are "using" our religion. Religious action is "practical" in the sense that it has concrete consequences which may lead us to reevaluate our commitments, and in the sense that we can experiment in order to discover those means which are most effective in helping us worship, work toward our ideals, and communicate our faith. But at the fundamental level of commitment, the "experimental attitude" is not compatible with "the religious attitude." A mature religious faith consists in wholehearted (though not close-minded) commitment to that which affects us as right and true and good. It does not consist in choosing something *because* it gives us peace of mind or leads us into religious ecstasy. To be sure, commitment to what affects us as right and true and good may give us peace of mind and bring about occasional religious highs, but the commitment is not for the sake of these things and is maintained in spite of their absence.

## TOWARD A FAITH OF YOUR OWN

The upshot of all that I have been saying is that you and I need a fully self-conscious, evaluated faith of our own in order to live at the highest level of human existence. Such a faith cannot be taken over from others in a mechanical way. An authentic faith is inevitably constructed or appropriated in a highly personal manner, so that even when the *content* of two persons' faiths is basically the same—e.g., two Roman Catholics— the *accents* may differ greatly. Wilfred Cantwell Smith does an excellent job in his *The Meaning and End of Religion* of arguing for the inevitable uniqueness of religious faith.[1] He begins by arguing that there is no such thing as religion, in the sense of "a certain kind of thing." The word "religion" has meant many, many different things at different times in history and during any given period of history. Ultimately, then, there is no singular thing that can be designated correctly by the word "religion." There is only your faith and her faith and his faith and my faith. Smith becomes more specific and argues that there is no such thing as Hinduism or Judaism, either! What justifies our calling two persons Hindus, and what justifies their calling themselves Hindus, is not that their faiths are identical or that they perform the same religious acts or that they belong to the same "thing." Two Hindus may not be identical or even clearly similar in any of these ways. Rather, we identify them and they identify themselves as Hindus because of their common participation in that tradition of litera- ture, ideas, practices, and rituals to which we refer by the term "Hinduism." But Hinduism, according to this usage, is not a clear-cut thing with well- defined boundaries by means of which it can be determined whether someone is inside it or not. Just where Hinduism begins and where it ends, just what are the necessary and sufficient conditions of being a Hindu, are highly disputable questions. The same dispute applies to perhaps every other religion.

To be sure, in nearly every religious tradition, there are groups that claim to be the only legitimate representative of that tradition. Such groups should be listened to earnestly, because one may be right. But until a person is satisfied that one group is the only legitimate representative of that tradition, he must—if he wants to identify himself with that tradition— draw deeply and broadly from its resources and create his own personalized commitment and participation. The person who does this may meet a group that says to him, "If you don't believe as we do, then not only do you not have the truth, but you shouldn't identify yourself (or think of yourself) as an $X$ (whatever the religion might be)." The practical thrust of such a group is to force the individual to choose their brand of $X$ or to reject $X$ altogether. But even if such a group is correct that its position is true and all others false, it does not follow that an individual who is not able to agree in good conscience with that contention should abjure his perception of himself as an $X$-ist of some sort. He knows whence he receives his greatest sense of inspiration—riddled though it may be with questions and gaps—and he should not allow anyone or anything but his own personal growth to dispossess him of his sense of being an $X$-ist rather than a $Y$-ist!

We do not, then, possess Buddhism, Christianity, Islam, and so on in some clear-cut, well-defined form. All we have for certain are the faiths of the individuals who participate in these various traditions. Such faiths, when they are living, dynamic faiths, are inescapably personalized, and should be. In order to make this point clear, Smith distinguishes between *personal faith* and *cumulative tradition*. "Cumulative tradition" refers to all things of a religious nature that are public and transmissible: for example, buildings for worship, symbols, art, creeds, music, rituals, literature, and dances. These are things we have in common because of their external, physical nature. Moreover, they can be passed on relatively unchanged from generation to generation. Faith, by contrast, is not external but internal. Nor is it the same thing from person to person, as the Nicene Creed is from church to church. Consider identical twins raised by the same parents in the same church or temple. Smith's point would be that they share the same cumulative tradition—they hear the same chants, sing the same hymns, read the same readings, perform the same symbolic acts, and so on. Yet, their faiths will be different because faith is not something that is impressed upon us from the outside. Rather, it is the result of our *personal appropriation* of the impact of our cumulative tradition upon us, and, of course, of the impact of our own thoughts and of other traditions upon us as we are exposed to them. John Dewey explains in his *Individualism Old and New* that individuality is a *distinctive* way of *feeling* the impacts of the world upon us and of *reacting* to them. As individuals, each of us *feels* differently the impacts of our religious learning, and consequently each of us *reacts* differently, be it ever so slightly—rejecting or being indifferent to that which others treasure, treasuring that which others are indifferent to or reject, cherishing more intensely or less intensely than others that which all cherish in common.

It is only natural that the materials for our faith are drawn first from the religious tradition in which we have been reared—if, indeed, we have been reared in any religious tradition at all. It would be foolish, however, to turn away from the lure of other traditions once we are exposed to them. It would be foolish also to reject the religious tradition of our childhood simply because it *is* the religious tradition of our childhood! Our response to the religious tradition that is passed on to us should not be unreflective acceptance or unreflective rejection, but appreciative and critical investigation and personalized appropriation.

An aside about religious education seems appropriate here. One of the saddest ironies of history is the extent to which adults intent on passing their religious heritage to children actually create in the children an intense dislike for the heritage. In my religion courses, I frequently invite students to write a personal statement of their religious beliefs, and the students often begin with an autobiographical account of their religious background. Frequently they share with me the extent to which they were bored to intense dislike of their religious heritage by their religious education. What a tragedy, especially given the good intentions and many volunteer hours invested by the teachers. Perhaps no religious education would be better than one that is counterproductive? Some people object to religious education not because it is counterproductive, but because they believe it unfairly biases a child in favor of one religion and against the others. It would be better, they say, for parents to give their children no religious education at all, so that when they reach maturity they can make an unbiased choice among the established religions or construct a religion of their own. That, of course, assumes a narrower definition of religion than the one with which we are operating. Further, there is a sense in which people must be *sensitized* to religious matters in order that they can make a mature choice, even as people must be sensitized to music before they can appreciate it fully or make sophisticated decisions about it. Personally, I can think of no adequate way to come to understand what religion is all about other than being *a part* of a religious tradition. The person who has participated in the Jewish heritage from childhood is, it seems to me, in an infinitely better position to evaluate *other* religious traditions than is a person who has never participated in any religious tradition but has only read about them. Some of my students have been reared in isolation from self-conscious religion and with the idea that religion is something "out there" about which they will make a decision when they become adults. Some of these students have expressed their regret to me that their parents had reared them this way, for they felt that a void had been left in their lives. First, they had been misled into thinking that religion is something "out there" and is, therefore, an optional part of human existence. Second, they had not been prepared to make an educated choice when the time for choosing did come. And, I must add, religious education, as aesthetic education, must involve the body and emotions as well as the intellect. Hence, it is difficult to see how it can be carried out effectively apart from actual immersion in some religious context—whether it is an ancient and elaborate one, such as Orthodox Christianity, or a new and simple one, such as an anti-institutional parent might create.

Further, not only should each individual be raised in a self-conscious religious tradition (even if it is a tradition that begins with the individual's parents), but the *entire* tradition should be passed on to the individual so that the individual can experience the full range of its richness. The older generation *owes* this opportunity to the younger generation. Professor Richard Rubenstein, the Jewish theologian to whom I am indebted for this insight, makes his point in the following words: "Jews are free to accept or reject all or part of the Torah as individuals. Freedom carries with it the responsibility that each generation make its own commitments in the light of its insights, while leaving the inherited corpus of tradition intact for subsequent generations."[2] Liberalism in religious education tends, by contrast, to impoverish the student by transmitting to the student only the convictions of the teacher and those portions of the heritage which back up his convictions. This tends to lead to a decrease in what is transmitted. To be sure, it is appropriate for the teacher to share his own insights and convictions with the student, but the student should be provided the entire body of material against which those convictions were arrived at so that he (the student) can discover whether *he* finds the same things or other things more important and convincing. Rubenstein is himself a Jewish atheist. Nonetheless, he writes with regard to the 613 commandments in the Torah, "I hope it will be possible for subsequent generations to confront all 613 commandments in the light of the insights of their time in order to decide what sector is meaningful for them. I seriously doubt that they will respond as we have."[3] Rubenstein recommends, then, that each generation should be confronted with the whole heritage, but that each member of that generation should be left free to determine his personal response to that heritage. This seems to me a wise recommendation for every religion, for though it places a burden on the adults who must carry it out, it provides maximal advantages to the young as they enter into their heritage and begin to decide their place in it.

Religious faith, then, is inevitably personalized to some extent, large or small. Abraham Maslow describes well the person whose faith is almost completely individualized. "From the point of view of the peak-experiencer," he writes,

> each person has his own private religion, which he develops out of his own private revelations in which are revealed to him his own private myths and symbols, rituals and ceremonials, which may be of the profoundest meaning to him personally and yet completely idiosyncratic, i.e., of no meaning to anyone else.[4]

At the other extreme of the spectrum is the person whose faith consists of personal appropriation of his parents' faith in its entirety. Most of us fall somewhere between these two extremes, our faith being the result of a more even balance between our own insights and what we have acquired from our religious nurture. While I do not agree with Maslow that the private religion of the peaker is what we should all strive for (I'm much more of a community person myself), I do agree with him that any faith worth having must be personal. It must be something that *happens within us* and is *nurtured by us*. As Carl Jung puts it, religious faith is *loyalty to one's own experience.*[5] It is concern for, confidence in, and commitment to your own deepest experiences—which may or may not be reinforced by the religious institution in which you were reared or, indeed, by any existing institution. People who are "looking for a religion" are sometimes, I think, looking not for a religion—that they have already in a private sense—but for a group of people who embody to a significant extent that which is already the seeker's religion, whether it be naturalistic humanism, transcendentalism, or theism (each of which will be discussed shortly). In order to cultivate your own faith, you are going to have to spend time in solitary reflection *identifying* your deepest experiences, *clarifying* them, *taking direction* from them, and *moving toward* yet further such experiences. Again, it's important to remember that such experiences can come from reflection upon events in which you have not participated and from ideas you did not originate, as well as from those in which you did participate and which you did originate. That is, you can benefit from, for example, the experiences and reflections recorded in the *Bhagavad-Gita* or the Bible, as well as from your own experiences and insights. Both types of experience are worthy of thoughtful consideration.

## NATURALISM, TRANSCENDENTALISM, AND THEISM

William James wrote a book titled, *Varieties of Religious Experience;* G. H. von Wright wrote *The Varieties of Goodness;* another book could well be written titled, "Varieties of Religious Faith." Yet, in spite of the endless variations of faith, I would like to suggest in closing that there are three fundamental modes of faith which have dominated the history of mankind, both East and West: the *naturalistic* mode, the *transcendentalist* mode, and the *theistic* mode. *Religious naturalism* is characteristic of atheistic humanists both East and West. For the religious naturalist, Nature—that which is presented to us by our senses, science, and ordinary introspection—is the whole of reality (though extraordinary experiences sometimes mislead us into thinking otherwise). The ultimate good is earthly happiness—often conceived of as some combination of physical health, material comfort, meaningful work, invigorating challenges, refreshing leisure, and intimate friends. The means to such happiness is human activity based on scientific knowledge of nature, self, and society.

For the *transcendentalist,* Nature is not the whole of reality. Indeed, it is only a veil we must penetrate in order to reach the One of which all things are a part. All things are part of the One as a wave is part of the ocean. The appearance of individuality, uniqueness, and separateness is an illusion. The truth is that you and I and all things are homogeneous with the One, even as the waves are one with the ocean. Hence, the ultimate good, according to the transcendentalist, consists in the blissful immersion and dissolution of our spirits in the One, which is Absolute Spirit. The consequent loss of individuality is not to be feared, for it is precisely the ego (our sense of separate individuality) that is responsible for our mental and spiritual confusion and suffering. By shedding the ego, we emerge from the chrysalis that has been preventing us from seeing reality as it is and becoming one with it. The way out of the chrysalis is disciplined meditation.

For the *theist* there is a creator and sustainer of reality who is personal in nature but eternally distinct from ourselves. Hence, there is no merger of the individual self with the Absolute Self. Rather, there is an eternal I-Thou relationship between God and the individual as there is between person and person. The ultimate good lies in the interaction of persons, including the Divine Person, with one another, and in the responsibility of persons, including the Divine Person, for one another. The means to this end are dialogue (including prayer), mutuality, and action.

With which of these three types of person do you feel most closely identified? What do you think of the other types? Is there any objective way of evaluating the relative merits of these three positions? Indeed, is there any *subjective* way of evaluating them? Can you think of another fundamental mode of faith that should be added here? I'm sure my trinity of modes is neither exhaustive nor satisfactory, but if it has served to heighten your consciousness of who you are and of what you might be, I am satisfied.

Finally, wherever you find yourself coming down—as naturalist, transcendentalist, theist, or something else—I hope you will never again think of religious faith as blind, cowardly assent to a set of propositions, but as intelligent, courageous consent to the best that you know. And lest you be lulled by all my talk of religion into thinking that I believe that religion is the most important thing there is, I say "for the record" that the focus of a healthy religion is not on religion but on God. "Those who make religion their god," warns Thomas Erskine of Linlathen, "will not have God for their religion." Far better it is, if we must choose, to have God than religion. But the choice hardly seems necessary or even possible, for it is through the forms of religion that we grasp and are grasped by God.

*"Now look what you've done!"*
Drawing by Lorenz; © 1971 The New Yorker Magazine, Inc.

## Footnotes

1. Wilfred Cantwell Smith, *The Meaning and End of Religion* (New York: The New American Library, 1963), esp. chaps. 6 and 7.
2. Richard Rubenstein, *After Auschwitz* (Indianapolis: The Bobbs-Merrill Company, Inc., 1966), p. 122.
3. Ibid., p. 146.
4. Abraham Maslow, *Religions, Values, and Peak-Experiences* (New York: The Viking Press, 1964), p. 28.
5. Carl Jung, *Psychology and Religion* (New Haven: Yale University Press, 1938), p. 52.

# For Further Reading

This bibliography is for readers who are just starting out in their study of religion. Hence, it is relatively short and most of the books are written on an introductory level. By limiting the bibliography in this way, it should serve well both those readers who can snatch only brief periods for reading and those readers who have not yet developed a capacity for lengthy or technical tomes. Readers who become intensely interested in a topic will find in nearly every category a book that contains an extensive bibliography on that topic. I hope you will be motivated to achieve a kind of "lay expertise" on at least one of the following topics. Because nearly all of these books and my own book embody a positive attitude toward religion, I have provided as the last category a section titled "Anti-Religious Literature."

## Introductions to Religion

MEAD, FRANK, *Handbook of Denominations in the United States* (5th ed.). Nashville: Abingdon Press, 1970. States briefly the beliefs, practices, and organization of nearly every religious group in the U.S. Good reference book.

MONK, ROBERT C., *et al., Exploring Religious Meaning.* Englewood Cliffs, N.J.: Prentice-Hall, 1973. An enjoyable blend of text, quotations, illustrations, and cartoons. Designed to keep the reader interested.

NOSS, JOHN B., *Man's Religions* (5th ed.). New York: The Macmillan Company, 1974. Comprehensive and excellent introduction to the religions of the world, primitive and modern, Eastern and Western.

SMITH, HUSTON, *Religions of Man.* New York: Harper & Row, Publishers, 1965. Very readable. Good place to start. Short chapters on seven religions, including Hinduism, Buddhism, Judaism, Christianity, and Islam.

STRENG, FREDERICK J., *et al.,* eds., *Ways of Being Religious: Readings for a New Approach to Religion.* Englewood Cliffs, N.J.: Prentice-Hall, 1973. Extensive collection of brief provocative selections from classical and contemporary authors.

## Phenomenology of Religion

BETTIS, JOSEPH D., ed., *Phenomenology of Religion: Eight Modern Descriptions of the Essence of Religion.* New York: Harper & Row, Publishers, 1969. Various points of view by leaders in the field.

ELIADE, MIRCEA, *The Sacred and the Profane: The Nature of Religion.* New York: Harcourt, Brace & World, 1959. Good introduction to a leading thinker who has written abundantly.

KING, WINSTON L., *Introduction to Religion: A Phenomenological Approach* (2nd ed.). New York: Harper & Row, Publishers, 1968. A coherent exposition from within a phenomenological-existentialist point of view of the nature and function of religion. Rarely speaks in generalities. Focuses on concrete aspects of specific religions.

OTTO, RUDOLF, *The Idea of the Holy.* New York: Oxford University Press, 1958. Classic example of phenomenological analysis.

VAN DER LEEUW, G., *Religion in Essence and Manifestation.* New York: Harper & Row, Publishers, 1963. A classic two-volume study. More wide-ranging than Otto's *Idea.*

## History of Religions

ELIADE, MIRCEA, AND JOSEPH KITAGAWA, eds., *History of Religions: Essays in Methodology.* Chicago: University of Chicago Press, 1959. Important statements by leaders in the field. Clear and valuable history of "the history of religions" school of thought in opening chapter by Kitagawa.

ELIADE, MIRCEA, *The Quest: History and Meaning in Religion.* Chicago: University of Chicago Press, 1969. A valuable set of papers by one of the leaders.

SMITH, WILFRED CANTWELL, *The Meaning and End of Religion.* New York: The New American Library, 1963. Another important scholar. Represents an important alternative to Eliade.

## Comparative Religion

ELIADE, MIRCEA, *Patterns in Comparative Religion.* New York: The New American Library, 1958. Very helpful chapter on the sacred and the profane, followed by studies of ways in which the sacred has been manifested in different cultures through the sky, water, woman, and other natural phenomena.

PYE, MICHAEL, *Comparative Religion: An Introduction through Source Materials.* New York: Harper & Row, Publishers, 1972. An interesting approach for the beginner, starting with an introduction to the nature of comparative religion. Illustrates seven religious topics such as "religion and general psychological factors," "religious concepts," etc. by means of quotations from many religions, primitive as well as modern.

SMITH, WILFRED CANTWELL, *The Faith of Other Men.* New York: The New American Library, 1963. A sensitive attempt to show why and how people of different faiths should relate to one another. Smith's conception of comparative religion set forth clearly and illustrated by six major religions.

WACH, JOACHIM, AND JOSEPH M. KITAGAWA, *The Comparative Study of Religions.* New York: Columbia University Press, 1958. Another pioneer in recent approaches to religion. (See also Noss and Smith under "Introductions to Religion.")

## Anthropology of Religion

LESSA, W. A., AND E. Z. VOGT, eds., *Reader in Comparative Religion: An Anthropological Approach* (3rd ed.). New York: Harper & Row, Publishers, 1972. Quite comprehensive. Widely used.

MALINOWSKI, B., *Magic, Science and Religion and Other Essays.* New York: Doubleday & Company, 1955. A classic study.

NORBECK, EDWARD, *Religion in Human Life: Anthropological Views.* New York: Holt, Rinehart and Winston, 1974. Serves as a brief introduction to anthropology of religion. Good bibliography.

## Sociology of Religion

BERGER, PETER L., *The Sacred Canopy: Elements of a Sociological Theory of Religion.* Garden City, N.Y.: Doubleday & Company, 1967. Quite recent, important approach. Seeks to understand how systems of religious belief and practice are generated from, maintained, and modified by social interaction. Rewarding, but not easy. The theoretical foundation for *The Sacred Canopy* is *The Social Construction of Reality—A Treatise in the Sociology of Knowledge* (1966) by Peter L. Berger and Thomas Luckmann. More difficult still. For an easy introduction to Berger's approach try his *Invitation to Sociology: A Human Perspective.* Garden City, N.Y.: Doubleday and Company, 1963. Luckmann's major statement on religion is *The Invisible Religion: The Problem of Religion in Modern Society* (New York: The Macmillan Company, 1967).

CAMPBELL, COLIN, *Toward A Sociology of Irreligion.* New York: Herder & Herder, 1972. An interesting attempt to distinguish irreligion from religion in order that the social factors in the generation of irreligion might be studied and the interactions between religious and irreligious groups might be submitted to sociological analysis.

GLOCK, CHARLES Y., ed., *Religion in Sociological Perspective: Essays in the Empirical Study of Religion.* Belmont, Calif.: Wadsworth Publishing Company, 1973. A book of readings by many authors on many topics in sociology of religion. Another valuable collection of readings for the beginner is *The Social Meanings of Religion: An Integrated Anthology,* ed. William M. Newman (Chicago: Rand McNally College Publishing Company, 1974).

GREELEY, ANDREW M., *The Denominational Society: A Sociological Approach to Religion in America.* Glenview, Ill.: Scott, Foresman and Company, 1972. A medium-length introduction to sociology of American religion. Intended to touch nerves and provoke thought.

O'DEA, THOMAS F., *The Sociology of Religion.* Englewood Cliffs, N.J.: Prentice-Hall, 1966. Excellent short introduction on subject. Includes sections on Emile Durkheim and Max Weber, classic figures in sociology of religion.

YINGER, J. MILTON, *Scientific Study of Religion.* New York: The Macmillan Company, 1970. Comprehensive, widely used text on the scientific study of religion, society, and the individual.

## Psychology of Religion

ALLPORT, GORDON W., *The Individual and His Religion.* New York: The Macmillan Company, 1950. Excellent essay on the role of religion in personal maturation.

FROMM, ERICH, *Psychoanalysis and Religion.* New York: Bantam Books, 1950. A thoughtful analysis by a religious naturalist.

HELFAER, PHILIP H., *The Psychology of Religious Doubt.* Boston: Beacon Press, 1972. Depth psychological case studies of numerous theological students representing different aspects and phases of religious doubt.

JUNG, CARL G., *Psychology and Religion.* New Haven: Yale University Press, 1938. Emphasizes symbolism and the unconscious mind. See also his *Modern Man in Search of a Soul.* New York: Harcourt Brace Jovanovich, 1955.

MASLOW, ABRAHAM H., *Religions, Values, and Peak-Experiences.* New York: The Viking Press, 1970. Fascinating attempt to reclaim mystical experience for naturalists.

SADLER, WILLIAM A., ed., *Personality and Religion: The Role of Religion in Personality Development.* New York: Harper & Row, Publishers, 1970. Valuable collection of statements from various psychologists.

SPINKS, G. STEPHENS, *Psychology and Religion.* Boston: Beacon Press, 1963. A single essay rather than a book of readings. Gives historical background as well as treating individual topics. Good place to start.

STRUNK, ORLO, ed., *Psychology of Religion.* Nashville: Abingdon Press, 1971. A book of readings with rare historical perspectives. Excellent bibliography.

VAN KAAM, ADRIAN, *Religion and Personality.* New York: Image Books, 1968. Interesting statement by a Catholic priest, psychologist, and director of the Institute of Man at Duquesne University. Existentialist point of view.

## Philosophy of Religion

CHISHOLM, RODERICK M., *Theory of Knowledge.* Englewood Cliffs, N.J.: Prentice-Hall, 1966. Good introduction to epistemology by a leader in that area.

HICK, JOHN, *Arguments for the Existence of God.* New York: Herder & Herder, 1971. Valuable, compact survey of most arguments. Concludes that theistic belief is rational in spite of the absence of proof.

HICK, JOHN, *Classical and Contemporary Readings in the Philosophy of Religion* (2nd ed.). Englewood Cliffs, N.J.: Prentice-Hall, 1970. Comprehensive collection of readings on many topics.

HICK, JOHN, *Philosophy of Religion* (2nd ed.). Englewood Cliffs, N.J.: Prentice-Hall, 1973. Excellent short introduction to philosophy of religion.

PLANTINGA, ALVIN, *God, Freedom, and Evil.* New York: Harper & Row, Publishers, 1974. The easiest introduction to a new and important approach to philosophy of religion.

TAYLOR, RICHARD, *Metaphysics* (2nd ed.). Englewood Cliffs, N.J.: Prentice-Hall, 1974. Very readable short introduction.

TENNANT, F. R., *Philosophical Theology* (2 vol.). New York: Cambridge University Press, 1969. Argues that theism is the world-view most strongly supported by all evidence available, including scientific evidence. Demanding but highly respected.

## Religious Existentialism

BLACKHAM, H. J., *Six Existentialist Thinkers.* New York: Harper & Row, Publishers, 1952. Good introduction. Covers Kierkegaard, Jaspers, and Marcel, as well as Nietzsche, Heidegger, and Sartre.

BUBER, MARTIN, *Eclipse of God.* New York: Harper & Row, Publishers, 1952. Demanding but rewarding. An easier introduction to Buber's thought than *I and Thou* (cited under "Theism").

HERBERG, WILL, *Judaism and Modern Man.* New York: Atheneum Press, 1951. A clear, sensitive, and comprehensive statement by a Jew who was a Communist. For an explanation of his conversion see "From Marxism to Judaism" in *Commentary* (January 1947).

JAMES, WILLIAM, *The Will to Believe and Other Essays in Popular Philosophy.* New York: Dover Publications, c. 1900. Very readable, provocative.

JASPERS, KARL, *Way to Wisdom.* New Haven: Yale University Press, 1951. The best introduction to a profound thinker.

KIERKEGAARD, SØREN, *Fear and Trembling,* trans. Walter Lowrie. Bnd. with *Sickness unto Death.* Princeton, N.J.: Princeton University Press, 1954. Excellent introduction to the major pioneer of recent religious existentialism.

LYNCH, WILLIAM F., S. J., *Images of Hope.* New York: Mentor-Omega Books (The New American Library), 1965. A readable and positive essay on the psychology and metaphysics of hope. Frequent illustrations from fiction. Extensive bibliography.

MARCEL, GABRIEL, *Creative Fidelity.* New York: The Noonday Press, 1964. Perhaps as good a place as any to dive into Marcel. Difficult but rewarding.

TILLICH, PAUL, *Dynamics of Faith.* New York: Harper & Row, Publishers, 1957. Excellent introduction to Tillich on faith.

DE UNAMUNO, MIGUEL, *Tragic Sense of Life.* New York: Dover Publications, 1921. Classic example of hope that refuses to yield as long as there is a possibility.

## Religious Naturalism

DEWEY, JOHN, *A Common Faith.* New Haven: Yale University Press, 1934. Excellent statement of the naturalist vision of human unity by "the dean of American philosophers."

*Fundamentals of Marxism-Leninism.* Moscow: Foreign Languages Publishing House, 1963. Comprehensive, authoritative statement of the philosophy and ideals of Marxism-Leninism according to Russian Communists.

HUXLEY, JULIAN, *Religion without Revelation.* New York: New American Library, 1957. A philosophy of evolutionary, scientific humanism by a distinguished British biologist.

LAMONT, CORLISS, *Philosophy of Humanism* (5th ed.). New York: Frederick Ungar Publishing Co., 1965. Up-to-date, comprehensive statement by a committed humanistic naturalist.

Unitarian-Universalism: see *The Unitarian Universalist Pocket Guide,* ed. Harry Barron Scholefield. Boston: Beacon Press, 1965; *Why I am a Unitarian Universalist,* by Jack Mendelsohn. Boston: Beacon Press, 1966. Also, "The Unitarian Universalists," a pamphlet published by Claretian Publications of Chicago, 1967. Scholefield and Mendelsohn are UU ministers. Pamphlet recommended highly by a UU minister.

WIEMAN, HENRY NELSON, *Man's Ultimate Commitment.* Carbondale, Ill.: Southern Illinois University, 1958. Fascinating attempt to modernize our concept of God. See also his *The Source of Human Good.* Carbondale, Ill.: Southern Illinois University Press, 1946.

## Transcendentalism

BURTT, E. A., ed., *The Teachings of the Compassionate Buddha.* New York: The New American Library, 1955. Sensitive selection of Buddhist literature with glossary of Buddhist terms.

CASTANEDA, CARLOS, *Don Juan Trilogy.* New York: Simon and Schuster, 1974. Fascinating account by an anthropologist of experiences that do not seem to fit into a naturalistic framework.

CHANG, GARMA C. C., *The Practice of Zen.* New York: Harper & Row, Publishers, 1959. Excellent introduction by a Chinese master.

DASS, RAM, *Be Here Now.* San Cristobal, New Mexico: Lama Foundation,

1971. Designed to hold reader's interest. Dass was formerly Dr. Richard Alpert, teacher of psychology at Harvard University.

JASPERS, KARL, *Way to Wisdom.* Cited earlier. Excellent example of the intellectualist's way to transcendental consciousness.

RADHAKRISHNAN, SARVEPALLI, *Hindu View of Life.* New York: The Macmillan Company, 1939. Excellent introduction by an outstanding Hindu thinker and person of action. See also his *Recovery of Faith.* Thompson, Conn.: InterCulture Associates, 1962.

*The Song of God: Bhagavad-Gita.* New York: The New American Library, 1951. Perhaps the most important single piece of Hindu literature. Short, engrossing.

SUZUKI, D. T., *An Introduction to Zen Buddhism.* New York: Grove Press, 1964. Very readable introduction. Forthright discussion of ways in which the Western mentality interferes with an appreciation of Zen. Foreword by Carl Jung.

WATTS, ALAN, *Joyous Cosmology.* New York: Random House, 1962. One of many books by a Westerner absorbed by eastern religion.

YOGANANDA, PARAMAHANSA, *Autobiography of a Yogi.* Los Angeles, Calif.: Self-Realization Fellowship, 1971. Fascinating personal account by an Indian.

# Theism

'ABD-AL-RAHMAN 'AZZĀM, *The Eternal Message of Muhammed.* New York: The New American Library, 1964. The substance and modern relevance of Islam explained by an Arab statesman and scholar.

BARTH, KARL, *Dogmatics in Outline.* New York: Harper & Row, Publishers, 1959. Perhaps the most influential Protestant theologian of this century. See also *Church Dogmatics: A Selection,* abr. ed. New York: Harper & Row, Publishers, n.d.

*The Bible.* The holy book of Jews and Christians alike. However, what the Jews refer to as their "Bible," Christians refer to as their "Old Testament," to which they add a "New Testament." Also, the Catholic Bible contains a few more documents than the Protestant Bible. Many translations by all three groups available.

BUBER, MARTIN, *I and Thou.* New York: Charles Scribner's Sons, 1970. Classic work by a Jewish philosopher. Examines the I–Thou relationship between God and person as well as between person and person.

GILSON, ETIENNE, *The Christian Philosophy of St. Thomas Aquinas.* New York: Random House, 1960. The ideas of Aquinas, Catholicism's main philosophical spokesman, explained by one of his most respected interpreters.

HESCHEL, ABRAHAM, *God in Search of Man: A Philosophy of Judaism.* New York: Harper & Row, Publishers, 1955. Rich and comprehensive statement by an orthodox Jew. See also his *Man Is Not Alone.* New York: Harper & Row, Publishers, 1966.

PICKTHALL, MOHAMMED M., trans., *The Meaning of the Glorious Koran.* New York: The New American Library, 1930. Valuable attempt by a Muslim to communicate the teachings of the Koran to those who do not read Arabic.

TILLICH, PAUL, *Systematic Theology.* Chicago: University of Chicago Press, 1963. The major protestant alternative to Barthian theology. Influential in philosophy and psychology as well as theology.

## Religious Experience

JAMES, WILLIAM, *The Varieties of Religious Experience.* New York: The Modern Library, 1902. Very readable, classic study with many examples.

OTTO, RUDOLF, *Mysticism: East and West.* New York: Meridian Books, 1932. Compares religious experiences from different religious traditions. Another classic.

SMITH, HUSTON, "Do Drugs Have Religious Import?", *Journal of Philosophy,* LXI, No. 18 (October 1, 1964). An examination of similarities between religious experience and drug-induced experience. Discusses the question, Can a genuine religious experience be induced by drugs? Reprinted in Streng's *Ways,* cited earlier. See also *Varieties of Psychedelic Experience,* R. E. Masters and Jean Houston. New York: Dell Publishing Company, 1967.

UNDERHILL, EVELYN, *Mysticism.* New York: E. P. Dutton & Co., 1911. Considered by many to be the best single study of mysticism.

ZAEHNER, ROBERT C., *Mysticism: Sacred and Profane.* New York: Oxford Galaxy Books, 1961. Rejects claims for the religious significance of drug-induced experiences. Discussed in H. Smith's article along with Aldous Huxley's *Doors of Perception.* New York: Harper & Row, Publishers, 1970, which affirms the religious validity of drug-induced experiences.

## Science and Religion

BARBOUR, IAN C., *Issues in Science and Religion.* New York: Harper & Row, Publishers, 1966. Comprehensive survey by a trained physicist who is also a philosopher/theologian.

BARBOUR, IAN C., *Myths, Models, and Paradigms.* New York: Harper & Row, Publishers, 1974. A more recent work of narrower scope. Examines, inter alia, the bearing on *religious* paradoxes of the acceptance of "paradox" (wave/particle complementarity) in physics.

SCHILLING, HAROLD K., *The New Consciousness in Science and Religion.* Philadelphia: United Church Press, 1973. Argues that the consciousness of mankind is being transformed in such a way that the old dichotomy of science and religion into two conflicting camps is being overcome.

STONER, PETER W., assisted by Robert C. Newman, *Science Speaks* (3rd ed.). Chicago: Moody Press, 1969. Argues that science confirms the credibility of the Bible. Compares the Genesis 1 creation story and the directions of recent astronomy.

## Immortality and Resurrection

GEACH, PETER, *God and the Soul.* New York: Schocken Books, 1969. An important statement by a philosopher who rejects reincarnation but believes in the possibility of resurrection.

LEWIS, HYWEL D., *The Self and Immortality*. New York: The Seabury Press, 1973. Good survey of the problem. Defends the tradition of Plato and Descartes and the meaningfulness of a disembodied soul.

NIEBUHR, RICHARD R., *Resurrection and Historical Reason*. New York: Charles Scribner's Sons, 1957. Defends a literal interpretation of the resurrection of Jesus.

PHILLIPS, D. Z., *Death and Immortality*. New York: St. Martin's Press, 1970. Argues that neither resurrection nor survival of death by the soul makes sense. A sensitive endeavor to invest "immortality" with humanistic meaning.

PLATO, *Phaedo*. A classic series of arguments by Socrates for the reality and indestructibility of the soul, as delivered to his friends visiting him in his jail cell just before his death sentence was carried out.

STENDAHL, KRISTER, ed., *Immortality and Resurrection*. New York: The Macmillan Company, 1965. Differences between the conceptions of immortality and resurrection in ancient Greece and in biblical Palestine investigated by four scholars.

## Autobiographies with a Religious Dimension

BONHOEFFER, DIETRICH, *Letters and Papers from Prison*, rev. ed. New York: The Macmillan Company, 1967. Gentle but outspoken German protestant theologian, imprisoned and executed by Nazis.

DASS, RAM, *Be Here Now*. Cited earlier. See opening section for story of an American Jewish psychologist's journey into India and Hinduism.

GANDHI, MOHANDAS K., *An Autobiography: The Story of My Experiments with Truth*. Boston: Beacon Press, 1957. Hindu lawyer, civil leader, and saint. Practitioner of "love-force." Frequently jailed, finally assassinated.

HAMMARSKJÖLD, DAG, *Markings*. New York: Alfred A. Knopf, 1964. Personal reflections by a former Secretary-General of the U.N.

KELLER, HELEN, *The Story of My Life*. New York: Dell Publishing Co., 1902. Totally deprived of sight and hearing at the age of nineteen months, yet developed a profound appreciation for religion. See also her later statement, *My Religion*. New York: The Swedenborg Foundation, 1960.

KING, MARTIN LUTHER, JR., *Stride Toward Freedom*. New York: Harper & Row, Publishers, 1958. Black civil rights leader in U.S. Followed Gandhi in advocating loving but aggressive nonviolence. Assaulted, jailed, assassinated.

KING, MARTIN LUTHER, JR., *Why We Can't Wait*. New York: The New American Library, 1963. Presents another segment of the black civil rights movement of which King was such a vital part in the 1950s and 1960s.

MALCOLM X, *The Autobiography of Malcolm X*. New York: Grove Press, 1965. From criminal to Black Muslim to orthodox Muslim. A fascinating story.

SCHWEITZER, ALBERT, *Out of My Life and Thought*. New York: The New American Library, 1933. A profound philosophy of life emerging from Schweitzer's account of his own many-sided development as musician, biblical scholar, philosopher, and missionary physician.

WATTS, ALAN, *In My Own Way: An Autobiography.* New York: Random House, 1972. Another testimony by a Westerner to the beauty of Hindu religion.

YOGANANDA, PARAMAHANSA, *Autobiography of a Yogi.* Cited earlier. Rich in detail and warmly human.

## Anti-Religious Literature

AYER, A. J., *Language, Truth, and Logic.* New York: Dover Publications, 1946. Argues that the concept of God is meaningless.

DEWEY, JOHN, *A Common Faith.* Cited earlier. Argues that there is no such thing as religious experience in the sense of a special kind of experience.

FEUERBACH, LUDWIG, *The Essence of Christianity.* New York: Harper & Row, Publishers, 1957. Important figure in development of modern atheism and communism. Argues that the idea of God is a projection of the human mind. (Frederick Ungar Publishing Co. publishes an abridgment.)

FREUD, SIGMUND, *The Future of an Illusion.* New York: Doubleday & Company, 1927. A forceful critique by means of psychological explanation. See also his *Civilization and Its Discontents,* James Strachey, ed. and trans. New York: W. W. Norton and Company, 1962; *Moses and Monotheism,* Katherine Jones, ed. Westminster, Md.: Random House, Inc., 1955; and *Totem and Taboo,* James Strachey, ed. New York: Norton, 1952.

MADDEN, EDWARD H., AND PETER H. HARE, *Evil and the Concept of God.* Springfield, Ill.: Charles C Thomas, Publishers, 1968. Argues that the enormity of evil proves that God does not exist.

MARX, KARL, AND FRIEDRICH ENGELS, *On Religion.* New York: Schocken Books, 1964. By the founders of modern communism. Explains religion as a form of alienation. Selections compiled in Moscow.

MATSON, WALLACE I., *The Existence of God.* Ithaca, N.Y.: Cornell University Press, 1965. Closely reasoned criticisms of arguments for the existence of God.

NIELSEN, KAI, *Contemporary Critiques of Religion.* New York: Seabury Press, 1972. Persistent critic of theistic belief. Concludes that it is no longer an option for rational persons.

NIELSEN, KAI, *Ethics without God.* Buffalo, N.Y.: Prometheus Books, 1973. Argues that the enterprise of ethics can get along perfectly well without God.

NIELSEN, KAI, *Skepticism.* New York: St. Martin's Press, 1973. Yet another of Nielsen's attacks on theism.

NIETZSCHE, FRIEDRICH W., *Thus Spake Zarathustra; Gay Science;* and *The Anti-Christ.* Most of these three works can be found in *The Portable Nietzsche,* ed. Walter Kaufmann. New York: The Viking Press, 1954. One of theism's harshest critics. Originated the statement: "God is dead." Explains religion as a form of weakness that is worthy only of being despised.

RUSSELL, BERTRAND, *Religion and Science.* New York: Oxford University Press, 1935. Reviews the history of the conflict of religion and science with a view to showing that religion is being replaced by science and should be.

RUSSELL, BERTRAND, *Why I Am Not a Christian.* New York: Simon and Schuster, 1957. Popular writings against religion, and especially Christianity. Points made forceful by author's stinging wit and authoritative tone.

SARTRE, JEAN-PAUL, *Existentialism and Human Emotions.* New York: Philosophical Library, 1957. Another withering blast at theism. Contains Sartre's lecture, "Existentialism as a Humanism," plus appropriate selections from *Being and Nothingness,* Hazel E. Barnes, trans. New York: Washington Square Press, 1966.

# Index